VALUE RETURNS

Wise Investing for the Next Decade and Beyond

Randy R. Beeman & James D. Schneider
Foreword by Tom Peters

Books are available for special promotions and premiums. For details, contact Special Markets, LINX, Corp., Box 613, Great Falls, VA 22066, or e-mail specialmarkets@linxcorp. com.

Book design by Paul Fitzgerald
Editing by Sandra Gurvis

Published by LINX

LINX, Corp.
Box 613
Great Falls, VA 22066
www.linxcorp.com

Printed in the United States of America

DEDICATION & ACKNOWLEDGEMENTS

The authors would like to dedicate this book to each and every client of the Wise Investor Group throughout the world. They have placed their trust in our team to guide them through the rough seas of the current secular bear market, and they count on us to help them reach the safety and security of the island of comfortable retirement. We greatly appreciate that trust, and every member of our team works diligently every day to be worthy of their confidence.

We would like to acknowledge Steve Eunpu for helping us make the dream of writing a book become reality, Sandra Gurvis for taking our random thoughts and turning them into coherent text, Pat Nowak for spending hours reviewing the content, and last, but certainly not least, our families—Bethann, Kasey, and Carol—for their understanding during the long hours, evenings, and weekends away from them while we completed this work.

DISCLAIMER

This book is provided for informational purposes and should not be used as the sole basis for making any investment decision.

While we are strong adherents of value investing, all investments are subject to risk, and an investor should have a thorough understanding of the risks of any stock, bond, or fund prior to investing in it. While some investors have the time and resources to make investment decisions for themselves, it is strongly recommended that the advice of a financial professional be sought prior to investing.

There is no guarantee that using a strategy, such as dollar cost averaging, will ultimately be profitable. Further, these are strategies that typically have the greatest potential for success if they can be implemented over a long period of time, and investors should consider their risk tolerance, diversification needs, and ability to continue to invest even during volatile markets.

Past performance is not a guarantee of future results, and diversification does not ensure against loss.

TABLE OF CONTENTS

Part 1—Value Investing Yesterday and Today

Section I: Introduction to Value Investing

Section II: Rules for Successful Value Investing

Section III: Myths of Value Investing

Part 2—Value Investing Strategy

Section I: Tactical Value Investing

Section II: Qualities of Exceptional Companies

Part 3—The Times Have Changed

Section I: Things Are Different

Part 4—How to Invest Now

Section III: Tactical Investments

Part 5—Putting It All Together

Section I: Prepare for the Next Secular Bull Market

FOREWORD

By TOM PETERS

My claim to public attention came courtesy of co-authoring *In Search of Excellence* in 1982. The book was written amidst tough and unstable times for the American economy—and American companies were under unrelenting assault from the likes of Japanese carmakers. But my co-author, Bob Waterman, and I found some shining American lights, from McDonald's and Walmart to Hewlett Packard and Intel. Over the next three decades, most of these firms performed rather well and safely but not spectacularly outperformed the market as a whole.

The "magic" was that, well… there was no magic. These companies executed day in and day out on the basics. They honored the talents of their employees and thence brought forth unusual levels of commitment and care. They listened constantly and slavishly to their customers and were in intimate, hands-on touch with their markets. They were willing to try and test new things with little muss and fuss—and do more if their ideas worked and stem their losses in a flash if they didn't. And, above all, they behaved with noteworthy integrity and stayed ever true to their core values through thick and, especially, thin.

The sorts of characteristics that I admired (and continue to admire) in those stellar companies and others that I have researched in the intervening years are, not surprisingly, the characteristics that I admire in a financial advisor. I am not interested in "flashy"—in fact, I run from the word and deed like the plague. I want a constant and restless probing of the upside, a willingness to react with dispatch to changing circumstances—but a general bias toward conservatism. Decent growth + exceptional security are my aim and, of course, a standard of transparency and integrity that's "off the charts."

In preparing my lectures and writing products, I scour the pages of history for commentaries that encapsulate the views I've discovered in researching the long-term excellent companies. None is better or more apt than this assertion by Napoleon Bonaparte:

> *"The art of war does not require complicated maneuvers; the simplest are the best and common sense is fundamental. From which one might wonder how it is generals make blunders; it is because they try to be clever."*

Common sense is, of course, among the most uncommon and thence most highly cherished virtues. I sleep well and look forward to the future, even amidst these madcap times, with a security I had not imagined possible. And I believe that what you will discover in these pages will go a long way toward explaining the basis for my confidence in my financial wellbeing.

Tom Peters
Author and Lecturer
West Tinmouth, Vermont

INTRODUCTION
"It's Different This Time"

These are typically the four most dangerous words uttered when describing the rationale for an investment or the underlying economic and market environment. The truth is, it's hardly ever really different, but at high and low market extremes, the delusional proclamation that "This time is different" always seems to surface. It was (supposedly) different in 1929 and 2000. During both periods, the extreme expansion of equity market valuations was based on speculative activity surrounding the development of new technologies. The 1920s saw the widespread introduction of an amazing range of innovations, including radio, automobiles, aviation, and the deployment of electrical power grids. The late 1990s was the decade when Internet and e-commerce technologies emerged. During both periods, market pundits widely proclaimed that the traditional business model was obsolete and the development of new technology would lead to sustained economic expansion without recessionary declines—the economic equivalent of continually sailing in calm waters on a beautiful sunny day. Oops, guess they missed the storm looming on the horizon—the 1929 Wall Street crash and the Great Recession of the 21ˢᵗ century—and it wasn't that different after all.

But perhaps something actually did change, and it really was different at the end of both periods—just not the way pundits expected. With the benefit of hindsight, we can see that a change did occur in 1929, which meant the following two decades would result in a greatly altered investing climate compared to the previous two decades. The peak of the equity market in 1929 signaled the beginning of a multi-decade phase known as a secular bear market, a prolonged period during which the appreciation of the equity market tends to underperform the very long-term averages. These extended sideways- or downward-trending markets are caused by a combination of excess valuation and prolonged economic distress. If you examine the equity market over the last decade, it is clear that the top of the equity market in 2000 heralded the start of another secular bear market. If it matches historical averages, this secular period could extend well into 2015-17.

The two decades following 1929 represented a dramatically different climate for investors participating in equity markets. The same is true for investors who have been attempting to steer their way through the volatility of the last decade. Secular bear periods are a much more hostile investing climate and require investors to reassess their perceptions of risk, reward, allocation, and diversification. Luckily, we have the benefit of similar historical periods to use as reference points to navigate our investment sailboats through the surrounding rough, stormy seas.

By examining the rules of successful value investing; information on the qualities of exceptional companies, diversification, and allocation; strategic vs. tactical investments; and more, we hope this text will aid you in your journey.

Randy R. Beeman
James D. Schneider

PART 1
VALUE INVESTING
YESTERDAY & TODAY

Value Returns

SECTION I:

Introduction to Value Investing

1: A Brief History

Value investing has a long, rich history. Hundreds of years ago, wealthy British families bought financial instruments called gilts, which were essentially bonds, to provide income for their families—hence, the term "gilt-edged." The purchase price was based on the dividends to be earned and was determined by figuring a percentage of the future income generated by the gilt.

Investors started buying stocks, also hundreds of years ago, for similar reasons. The stock was purchased at a price based on the expected dividend, but unlike bonds/gilts, stocks don't mature. So, as long as the company was around, the investor received the dividend payment.

In both cases, investors determined if the particular bond or stock was a good investment by examining it from a value point of view. This is known as value investing and involves buying an asset that produces a stream of income considered reasonable today in relation to that company's current price. In other words, they are buying something today that based on their research, they expect will provide a stream of income in the future.

So, investors started moving from buying gilts/bonds to buying stocks that paid relatively high dividends. As recently as the 1950s, stocks paid higher dividends than bonds because they were deemed to be riskier; investors wanted to be compensated for the increased risk.

Today, however, dividend yields are much lower than in the past. The decline in dividends parallels that of American industry, as these companies traditionally paid high dividends. In the latter part of the 20th century, the mindset changed, as investors began to buy stocks more for their capital appreciation potential—that is, the amount of increase found in the principal value and/or the price per unit of a share over a given period of time—and less for the income generated by the dividends.

The important role of dividends in providing total returns on a long-term basis has been largely forgotten. From 1926 to 2009, the stock market had a total return of 9.6 percent per year with dividends making up 4.1 percent, or over 40 percent, of that return.[1] In other words, without a dividend, investors would have, in effect, only received an average of a 5.5 percent return on their investment (ROI).

Dividends and dividend growth matters to a value investor, especially during bear markets (see box).

To Market, to Market: Bear vs. Bull

When you hear talk about a bear market, that means a prolonged period in which valuations fall, which is accompanied by widespread pessimism. The term "bear" has been used in a financial context since at least the early 18th century and may have originated from traders who sold bear skins with the expectations that prices would fall in the future.

Bear markets usually occur when the economy is in a recession and unemployment is high or

---

1 Bloomberg, Standard & Poors, The Wise Investor Group

when inflation is rising quickly. During most bear markets, the volatility of prices increase, and the range of fluctuations also tend to widen. This increasing volatility causes many investors to experience heightened anxiety about the safety of their investments. The most famous bear market in U.S. history was the Great Depression when the equity market peaked in 1929 and didn't reach a new high again for 25 years! Recent times have inspired comparisons to that dark financial period.

A bull market is the exact opposite of a bear market. Marked by a prolonged period in which valuations rise faster than their historical average, bull markets can happen as a result of an economic recovery or boom or because of investor psychology. The longest and most famous bull market began in the early 1980s but really pushed higher in the '90s when U.S. equity markets grew at their fastest pace ever. Shorter bull markets occurred in the 1920s and during the '60s.

Source: www.investorwords.com

2: Value vs. Growth Investing

The stock market has two investing styles: value and growth. Basically, value investors want to own great companies at cheap or attractive prices and at below-average price to earnings ratio (P/Es)—basically, the price of the stock divided by the earnings per share. Value investors also want these companies to have significant moats around their businesses as well as to generate large amounts of free cash flow. A competitive advantage over other companies in the same industry, a moat can either be cost-related, such as producing a good or service more cheaply than others, or intangible, such as brand recognition. Examples of businesses with moat characteristics are McDonald's, Procter & Gamble, Johnson & Johnson, and Coca-Cola.

The primary tenets of value investing were outlined in *Security Analysis*, a scholarly text written by Benjamin Graham and David Dodd in 1934. A later, less textbook-oriented version was also published as *The Intelligent Investor*. In essence, Graham and Dodd encouraged investors to compare the value of the operating business (its assets and cash flow) to the price of its stock. An opportunistic value occurred when the stock could be bought for less than the value of the assets (or book value). This provides a substantial margin of safety, like wearing a belt and suspenders to hold up your pants. The last thing you want if your suspenders break is to find your pants at your ankles. These opportunities are much less plentiful today, but astute value investors can still find them in solid companies.

Growth investors want to buy companies that are expanding their earnings or expected earnings at a rapid rate, often irrespective of the stock's price or valuation. In essence, they are buying a stock today that is perceived to be growing at a fast pace, regardless of whether it might eventually fall in value. In their mindset, this potential overvaluation is irrelevant because tomorrow somebody else might purchase the stock at an even higher valuation. Thus, investors are frequently attracted to a specific area at any one point in time, such as the biotechs in the early '90s or the technology stocks in 1998-1999 or the residential real estate market from 2002-2006. And everyone knows what happened to those assets! **As Benjamin Graham, the late economist and value investing pioneer, observed, "Wall Street people learn nothing and forget everything."**

3: *Value Investing 101*

Discussions of investing styles in terms of companies and generating free cash flow may be confusing for some people, particularly those who are new to investing. So let's look at value investing a different way. Once you understand the basics, you can apply the principles anywhere.

Suppose you wanted to buy a Honda Accord. If you saw it selling for $80,000, you probably wouldn't be interested and would likely remain so even if the price was marked down 50 percent to $40,000. However, you might seriously consider purchasing a fully loaded new Accord for $20,000, particularly if it lists for over $25,000. In other words, you want to buy quality at a good price and value. The better the quality and/or the lower the price, the more likely you are to believe that you are getting a very good value. And that's what value investors do—find quality companies to invest in at a low enough price to make it worthwhile.

During a sale, people flock to grocery and department stores, but have you ever heard of anyone going to a store manager and saying they want a particular suit but only if the price was to rise by 10 percent, thus proving how desirable it is? But when it comes to investing in stocks, people do exactly that! Growth investors shun attractive companies whose stock is selling for a discount but flock to stocks that have shot up as if such momentum will continue unabated. This impetus cannot last forever since such investors are buying stock at increasingly expensive prices.

So if the price of the Honda Accord were to accelerate as quickly as the vehicle itself can, say from $25,000 to $30,000 to $50,000, would that make it more desirable? Not for most of us!

This is why value investors want to buy a dollar's worth of goods for 80 or 70 cents with the belief that the intrinsic value will be recognized and the price will rise to at least a dollar. In a bull or expanding market, the price might rise to over a dollar, yielding a very good profit. Growth investors tend to want to buy these goods after the price has already risen—from 70 cents to around or over a dollar—with the belief that it will continue to escalate and they can sell it at an even higher price. But as Gordon Gekko himself can attest, at some point the music stops.

4: *The Evolution of Value*

Author Benjamin Graham is also known as "the father of value investing." He practiced and taught the concept of intrinsic value—calculating the asset value of a business and only buying its stock if it traded at a discount to that valuation.

Graham's philosophy has evolved, with some updates, into

the deep value style practiced today by David Dreman and others. Deep value investing seeks to invest in stocks trading at a significant discount to their intrinsic, or book, value. A different take on the value philosophy was developed by entrepreneur Warren Buffett—who studied under Graham while at Columbia University in New York City—which added the requirement that the company must have specific quality characteristics. The company did not necessarily have to be trading at rock-bottom prices as long as it had a significant competitive moat or advantage, generated strong cash flow, and was "attractively" valued relative to the intrinsic value.

Within the last few decades, a third evolution of the value philosophy has developed. This value evolution espouses the importance of various quality criteria over the necessity that the stock be trading at a sharp discount to its intrinsic value. This merging of the elements of both value and growth styles is sometimes called "growth at a reasonable price" (GARP) and is practiced by successful financial investment managers like Bill Miller and others. If you think of the value style as a large tree, then Graham would represent the roots with the variations in execution represented by branches through Buffett, Dreman, and Miller.

(BUFFETT)

(DREMAN)

(MILLER)

(GRAHAM)

5: **Which Works Best?**

If you buy a good stock that's cheap, it has a greater chance of increasing in value, as it has an increasing price-to-earnings ratio (P/E) and provides much higher returns than a stock that's initially expensive. All else being equal, a low P/E stock has greater upside potential and lower downside risk than a high P/E stock; it makes common sense to buy something that's less costly. Investors often frantically get rid of companies with temporary problems so that the price of the stocks become a bargain. Thus, when the stock market declines, value stocks, on balance, do not go down as much because investors have already discounted the stock price. Hence, value stocks' relatively limited downside can help provide a solid base for the average investor's portfolio.

Studies show that over the long term, value almost always significantly outperforms growth. The paradox is that value is a more conservative investment strategy. In other words, growth dramatically underperforms and is riskier. Market capitalization combined with the distinction between value and growth can be a powerful appreciation engine. Consider the following:

- Since 1927, according to Ibbotson, Inc., small-cap value returned 14.1 percent a year vs. small-cap growth at 8.7 percent. That's 5.5 percent a year, an enormous difference. For large cap stocks, value expanded at 11.5 percent a year, while growth grew only at 9.1 percent.

"Caps" in a Nutshell

Market capitalization is calculated by multiplying the number of a company's shares outstanding by its stock price per share. Small cap stocks are those with a relatively small market capitalization, between $300 million and $2 billion, while large cap stocks have a market capitalization value of more than $10 billion. Large cap companies include Wal-Mart, Microsoft, and General Electric. However, the size of the "caps" can change with the times, varying among market participants and depending upon financial trends.

Source: www.investopedia.com

- From 1970 to 1997, the lowest P/E stocks returned 19 percent a year and the highest P/E stocks only returned 12 percent a year.[1]
- From July 1963 to March 1999, large cap value stocks outperformed large cap growth stocks by 29 percent with 10 percent less risk, while small cap value stocks

---

1 David Dreman, Contrarian Investment Strategies: *The Next Generation.*

outperformed small cap growth stocks by 70 percent with 20 percent less risk.[2]

- From January 1, 2000 to December 31, 2009, the S&P 500 large cap value stocks outperformed large cap growth stocks by 34 percent on a total return basis.[3]

Charting the annual performance of value versus growth generally shows a period of 2-3 years where growth outperforms value followed by 5-10 years of value outperforming growth. The longest stretch ever of growth outperforming value was between 1990 and 2000, especially between 1995 and 2000.

So, why would any investor buy something that's riskier and does much worse? Value investing—buying quality companies at below-average prices—not only gives you better returns in the long term but does so with less risk.

WISE INVESTING VALUE RULE NO.1

Why reinvent the wheel or try to play a hero? Stick with what works for the long haul. Value investing is time tested and works better with less risk.

---

2 William Bernstein, "'Value Stocks - Hidden Risk or Free Lunch," *Efficient Frontier*, September 1999.

3 Bloomberg, The Wise Investor Group.

Value Returns

SECTION II:

Rules for Successful Value Investing

6: *Why Do You Need Rules?*

During the last long-term equity bull market from 1982 to 2000, the percentage of Americans owning stocks expanded greatly. This was primarily due to the establishment and popularization of mutual funds; the introduction and widespread use of investment retirement accounts (IRAs) and 401(k)s; and Federal Reserve policies that focused on price stability, lower interest rates, and financial market growth. A literal deluge of financial information and the marketing of "successful" investment schemes accompanied an explosion in stock market participation.

During this period, the media, including newsletters, magazine articles, and Internet websites, abounded with "sure-fire" strategies, catering to the public's appetite for increasing wealth. People seemed to want to make up for lost time in their search for the financial Holy Grail, the plan that would get them rich overnight.

The truth, however, is that many such schemes wound up hurting much more than helping. Time-proven and useful ideas and strategies seemed to have gotten lost in the shuffle.

Because the decade since the equity market peak in 2000 has produced lackluster returns, a growing number of retiring baby boomers now realize they may not have enough "nest egg" to achieve their desired level of comfort and security. This has made them vulnerable to an increased risk-taking mentality and "get-rich-quick" pitches.

The next few chapters will define characteristics and qualities that have been successful for many value investors over time. Rather than being a map towards instant riches, the chapters represent a collection of investing ideas designed to teach you how to gradually grow wealth and reduce risk.

All investing is a balance between risk and reward; higher risk strategies, which have the potential to grow wealth rapidly, also have the potential to lose it just as quickly. And this latter point is an important one. In an effort to make up lost gains, some people may feel and act on the desire to throw caution to the wind and invest in high-risk ways to rapidly increase their financial holdings. Such action, unfortunately, also carries the chance of pushing them further behind, making them lose a large percentage of their current net worth, and forcing them to delay retirement even longer.

7: *Create a Financial "Road Map"*

Along with using his expression-filled face to convey nuggets of truth, the late, great **George Carlin was often quoted as saying, "Have you ever noticed that anyone driving faster than you is a maniac, and anyone driving slower than you is an idiot?"** We're all driving down the road to retirement, but some are going faster than others. Some may be acting recklessly by trying to take shortcuts, while others move so slowly they may not reach their destination before running out of gas. But each person traveling that highway needs a roadmap for their journey. Otherwise, how will you know whether you've reached your destination?

Similarly, how will you reach your goal of a secure retirement without a written financial plan and the proper asset allocation to balance risk and reward? Once you've constructed a financial plan, you'll know what is required of your investments to achieve your financial goals. Having a plan and defined allocation also helps control the emotions of fear and greed from dominating your investment decision-making process. A plan gives you a series of checkpoints so you can know if you are on or ahead of schedule or if you've fallen behind and need to correct the situation.

According to a study by the Employee Benefit Research Institute (EBRI), many investors remain unaware of how much they'll need to save for retirement.[4] Less than half of workers (46 percent) reported that they and/or their spouse tried to calculate the amount required for a comfortable retirement. Of those who did calculate, only 16 percent were confident about having enough money.

The following steps will help you construct a financial plan. While you can do some of the initial work yourself, at some point you will likely require the services of a professional planner or, at the very least, financial planning software. But as with any complicated and important undertaking, it's best to utilize an experienced and skilled professional if only because they can provide important (and potentially profitable) suggestions and can note problem areas and omissions before they become too severe.

Step One—Make a List

Using a piece of paper or your computer (and making sure you print out the list), make a list of your goals. What do you want to accomplish? What is important to you? Your plan should be goal-driven and specific. For example, instead of listing "Retirement" generically as a goal, you might write down "Retire by age 65 with enough income to replace 90

---

4 Employee Benefit Research Institute, www.ebri.org, http://www.ebri.org/pdf/PR.868.9Mar10.RCS-10.Final.pdf .

percent of my pre-retirement annual earnings." Knowing what you want is much better than having your retirement circumstances dictated to you. It is, after all, your future.

Retirement means different things to different people. For example, if you are a Baby Boomer, there is an 80 percent chance that you may keep working past the normal retirement age of 65, according to a study released by AARP.

So, what is important to you? I've heard things such as "I want to be financially independent by age X so I can do whatever I wish," or "I want to be able to take annual trips up the St. Lawrence River or to see Europe," or "I want to be able to make annual financial gifts to my grandkids," or even, "I still want to keep working but doing what I love rather than 'having' to be there."

Writing down your goals and clearly stating your intentions make the obligation(s) real. You've committed to something in writing and on paper. You've clarified your thoughts, making your goals and wishes concrete.

Financial planning has often been described as dreaming with deadlines. By putting deadlines on your goals, you are making a contract with yourself. As Steven Covey says, begin with the end in mind. By envisioning what you want, in essence, you create it mentally and set the stage for actuality.

Step Two—Inventory Your Assets

What do you have, and what is it worth? Make three columns for your investments—one column for taxable investments, like your traditional brokerage account; a second column for tax-deferred investments, such as 401(k)s and traditional IRAs; and a third column for your tax-exempt accounts, such as Roth IRAs and Roth 401(k)s. At a glance, you will be able to see the relative balance between the various tax treatments of your accounts.

Disproportionately larger balances in tax-deferred accounts represent a slightly higher risk because not everything in your 401(k) plan belongs to you. Uncle Sam is going to want his cut too. So, if tax rates go up in the future, you would have less spendable income from those accounts.

Step Three—Quantify Your Plans and Dreams

Consider how much you want to put into your investments. This will take careful consideration and is one of the major drivers of your plan's outcome. Also, it's an aspect that you can be in charge of. You can't control inflation, stock market returns, how long you live, or future tax rates, but when all things are equal, you can pretty much manage and predict how much you spend and save. A financial planner can also help you make realistic and achievable quantifications.

Step Four—Recognize the Realities

At the other end of the spectrum are things we have no control over. These include inflation, the rising cost of goods and services, which are signs of a healthy economy. Currently inflation is low by historical standards and could remain that way for several years, but your plan should encompass the future. I would suggest estimating inflation at higher levels than the current readings. Here again, the assistance of a professional planner can help you determine the proper protection.

Also, consider how long you think you will live. That may sound morbid, but it is essential for this type of planning. One way would be to look at longevity in your family. At what ages did your grandparents and (if applicable) your parents and other relatives pass away? Also consider actuarial tables, which show, based on age and sex, the probability that a person will die before his or her next birthday. But remember that these tables represent median numbers; that is, half of the people pass away before that actual number, while half keep on living after they reach that number. Which half you end up in will greatly influence the success of your plan!

Step Five—Review Your Progress

Periodically review your plan to make sure you are on track and are keeping it a top priority. What, if anything, has changed? You may have to make some adjustments to reach your goals, and it's also good to keep reminding yourself of your progress and/or any potential roadblocks.

Once you've completed the plan, allocate your investment assets to only take as much risk as necessary to achieve your goals. Allocation suggestions will be discussed later in the book.

Top 10 Indications You Need a Financial Plan

Taking a cue from the "Late Show with David Letterman," the following is a list, in descending order, of the top 10 reasons for having a financial plan. It's no joke, however, and all the reasons are important!

10. You notice your spouse's comments about the household's finances are becoming more frequent and pointed.

9. You don't know how much you spend or how much you'll want to spend in your future
8. You've just had another (or your first) child
7. You have no idea how you're going to pay for college for the above child
6. You've lost a lot of money in the stock market and have no idea why
5. You work at a job you dislike and see no end in sight
4. You have no insurance protection for anything
3. You've never constructed a financial plan
2. You go to bed thinking about your finances and wake up thinking about your finances
1. You don't know if you'll ever be able to retire

Source: Gregory S. Smith, CFP®, ChFC®, Managing Director, PWM Head Financial Planner, Wise Investor Group, Robert W. Baird & Co.

8: Be Value-Oriented

Most, if not all, of your equity portfolio should reflect value investing criteria. Numerous scholarly studies show value outperforms growth over the long term and does so with less risk. So why not focus on what works best?

The long-term average return from the broad stock market from 1926 to 2009 was 9.6 percent annually.[5] The return of the value component of the market during this period was 10.9 percent annually, while the growth component returned 8.9 percent per year on average. While a 2 percent differential in total annual return between the value and the growth styles of investing may seem insignificant, over such a long time period, it can make a substantial difference in the end market value of the investment.

Each of these total returns, however, was calculated under the assumption that an investor bought at the start of the 84-year period and held on to it for the entire time. In reality, most people rarely invest in that manner. Realistically, investments were probably made at certain time periods during the entire span due to either cash flow needs or the volatility of the market. Such fluctuations undoubtedly affected the investor's realized return either positively or negatively over the time period of the study.

Some investing texts propose and many professionals believe that having a mix of all types of investments (such as international, small cap, large cap, etc.), regardless of whether they are value or growth-oriented, will reduce risk and improve return. While proper diversification is important to manage risk, you still need to maintain a value-oriented bias in all components. Value works, so why diversify into something less attractive in the long term?

9: Practice Patience

Part of the mythology surrounding the American Dream involves investors who put their money into a small,

---

5 *Ibbotson SBBI, 2010 Classic Yearbook, Market Results for Stocks, Bonds, Bills, and Inflation* 1926–2009 (Chicago: Morningstar, 2010).

unknown stock near or at its low, somehow know to sell it near or at its top, and then plow their "enormous" profits into another stock that is near or at its low, repeating the same cycle over again. This gives rise to the notion of nonstop attention to your investments and trading your way to riches.

Unfortunately, that is not reality. Those who are content to grow their wealth slowly generally make out best in the long run. Almost all successful investors possess unusual quantities of patience. Your objective should be to buy not for a quick profit but to own great companies that compound their wealth on a long-term basis. Finding a great company, then turning around and selling it the next week for a small gain is counterproductive and a waste of time. **As investment expert Peter Lynch has said, "The key to making money in stocks is not to get scared out of them."**

Let compound interest, what Albert Einstein called the Eighth Wonder of the World, work in your favor. This also requires patience, which novice investors sometimes lack. If, for instance, they invest $2,000 and see it grow to $2,200 at the end of the year, many will feel frustrated with a "paltry" $200 gain instead of seeing it as a 10 percent increase, which could double their money in seven years. Even with the same percentage increase, the small dollar growth happens at the beginning, while the larger increase occurs towards the end.

Looking at this a different way—say that in a pond, a water lily duplicates itself once a day. After 30 days, the pond is totally covered with water lilies. This means that on Day 29, the pond is only half covered and that on Day 28, the pond is only one-quarter covered. Hence, three quarters of the growth came in the final two days! If the full (30-day) process was lacking only two days (such as starting late, quitting, or cutting it short early), three quarters of the growth would never take place!

10: Know Your Strengths and Limitations

This is very important, especially when building your portfolio. Know what you're good at and keep doing it. Stay away from what you dislike and are uncomfortable with. Ask yourself, do you really understand how to analyze stocks or bonds? If the answer is "no," then strongly consider hiring someone else to do it.

Find a money manager or a team of asset managers who follow your preferred investment style (hopefully, value) and have them help you construct a portfolio to reach your goals. This is the most logical choice for those with neither the time nor talent to do it themselves. The second best option is to use mutual funds.

No one can be good at everything. Discover your investment talents and comfort zones. Maybe you are best at evaluating small companies, understanding mutual funds, or trading in collectibles. Along with giving you the confidence to buy and sell at the right times, knowing your strengths will keep you from making big mistakes and getting outside your area of competency. Knowing what you own and have invested in will provide you with the conviction to stay with or buy more of your investment when the markets and the media pundits say otherwise.

Without strong convictions, your emotions may drive you to get in and out at the wrong times, buying high and selling low, so be honest with yourself.

11: Don't Over Trade

Many novice investors trade stocks back and forth, taking a small profit here and there, thinking this is how veteran investors get rich. But, as discussed previously, such actions are a waste of time and money, as experienced investors know. Excessive trading can be very expensive, not only in terms of brokerage commissions but also due to the fact that as of this writing, short-term gains are taxed at higher rates than long-term gains. But even more important are the missed opportunities. It's tough to find a great company or investment; what is the sense of selling it after it gains only a couple of points?

Sometimes beginning investors see trading as a game of chance and companies like pieces on a Monopoly board. However, successful investors understand that they are buying part of an operating business. If they are to harvest the fruit of increased dividends, they must stay the course. If the company has a strong business model, its capital will appreciate, although it may take some time.

Short-term criteria can result in stocks moving all over the place. Factors can range from policy shifts in the Fed (see box), economic trends or news that may spook the market, or something totally unrelated to the long-term underlying fundamentals of that company.

Meet "The Fed"

"Fed" can mean a lot of things—FBI agent Eliot Ness comes immediately to mind—but in financial parlance, it refers to the Federal Reserve System, often referred to as the Federal Reserve or simply "the Fed," the central bank of the United States. It was created by Congress to provide the nation with a safer, more flexible, and more stable monetary and financial system. Over the years, its role has evolved and expanded.

Today, the Fed's responsibilities fall into four general areas:

- Conducting the nation's monetary policy by influencing money and credit conditions in the economy in pursuit of full employment and stable prices
- Supervising and regulating banking institutions to ensure the safety and soundness of the nation's banking and financial system and to protect the credit rights of consumers
- Maintaining the stability of the financial system and containing systemic risk that may arise in financial markets
- Providing certain financial services to the U.S. government, the public, financial institutions,

and foreign official institutions, including playing a major role in operating the nation's payments systems.

The Federal Reserve System has a structure designed by Congress to give it a broad perspective on the economy and on economic activity all over the United States. It is composed basically of a central governmental agency—the Board of Governors— in Washington, DC, and twelve regional Federal Reserve Banks located in major cities throughout the nation. These components share responsibility for supervising and regulating certain financial institutions and activities, for providing banking services to depository institutions and to the Federal government, and for ensuring that consumers receive adequate information and fair treatment in their business with the banking system.

Source: www.federalreserve.gov

On a long-term basis, stocks tend to trade at or around their earnings growth rate; after all, you are buying that company today to share in those future earnings. If you went out and purchased a plumbing business today, you would expect to share in its future earnings because you own it. The same is true when you buy stocks if you are approaching it as an investor as opposed to a speculator who trades in the stock for a few points.

Being a successful long-term investor involves understanding that you are buying actual operating businesses and that you are investing in them just like you would plant crops for harvest. You are putting in the time now to cultivate their future growth.

The goal for these investments is to bear fruit when you retire by giving you increased dividend yields and earnings as the stock appreciates over time. Nurturing your investments will provide the potential for the increased dividends and capital appreciation that come from owning part of a fine quality business.

12: Buy On Sale

In real life, people don't go down to Saks, Nordstrom's, or Hecht's because they got a flier in the mail saying prices have been marked up 50 percent. Yet this happens all the time in the stock market. Growth investors wait until the stock has already gone up 50-100 percent, and then they say it's time to buy it. That makes no sense; that's when we would sell it!

We are value investors not just because it works but because it fits our personalities. If we're looking at anything—a suit or pair of shoes—we want good value. Sometimes it drives our wives crazy. They say that we never pay retail for anything, but we need to feel like we're getting a deal and a value. So "value investing" extends into all parts of our lives and more than just the stock market!

Be just as frugal with your stocks as you would be in purchasing a new car, clothes, or anything else. Would you rather get a suit on sale or one marked up 30 percent? If your answer is the former, why wait to buy a stock that you find attractive only after it's gone up, say, 30 percent? Unfortunately, many novice investors take the attitude that if a stock's price is falling, then no one wants it, and something is wrong, while if a stock's price is rising, then it's a winner, and let's all jump aboard ship (even if it might be the *Titanic*)! Sometimes a falling stock price can be a warning signal, but in other cases it's indicative of a temporary problem, thus making it a good bargain. For example, stocks often sell off in the short term if a quarterly earnings report fails to meet or exceed the market's expectations only to rebound in a future quarter once the longer term growth goals are realized.

If a particular industry looks promising, then buy the most inexpensive superior company in that industry (in this case, "inexpensive" does not refer to its price but to its value relative to the price). You want to comparison shop.

So if, for instance, you are looking at oil stocks, compare one oil stock to another rather than to another stock in a different industry.

13: *Get Good Advice and Educate Yourself*

Be discerning when you seek advice. Would you get medical opinions from the plumber or ask the person who delivers your newspaper about car repair? The same is true of value investing; if you want to learn about it, get information from the experts. **Benjamin Franklin said it best, "An investment in knowledge always pays the best interest."**

This includes reading books by successful investors, such as Sir John Templeton, Warren Buffett, Benjamin Graham, and David Dreman. Begin by studying the writings of Benjamin Graham. His book, *Security Analysis*, written with David Dodd, was first published in 1934, and is now in its sixth edition. As briefly mentioned before, Graham is also the author of *The Intelligent Investor*, published in 1949, which is also still in print in a current edition. Both books are considered classics and fundamental to an education in value investing.

Another value investment expert is David Dreman. He's nearly as well known in the value circles for his "contrarian" approach, which involves buying stocks when prices fall despite any overriding instincts to do the opposite. His recent book, *Contrarian Investment Strategies for the Next Generation*, is also essential reading for value investors. Dreman explains in clear, detailed language why the value-investing process works and why it provides better returns with less risk.

Financial publications, such as the *Wall Street Journal, Barron's, Outstanding Investors Digest*, and *Forbes,* contain a great deal of useful information and should be read on a regular basis, so you know what's going on in the marketplace. Also, find out what managers are doing at leading value-oriented investment houses, such as Longleaf, Tweedy Browne, Sequoia, and Legg-Mason Value Trust. You can pick up on their ideas, then do your own investigations by looking at their most recent holdings. Warren Buffett calls this strategy of mimicking the trades of well-known and historically successful investors "coat-tailing."

You can use these suggestions as a start but also develop your own list of trusted sources and stick to it. However, also remember there's a lot of bad advice out there, so stick to the sources you trust. If the focus seems to be on growth investing, panic trading, and get-rich-quick schemes, then it's time to close the pages or turn off the computer.

14: Avoid Focusing on the Short Term

Warren Buffett, paraphrasing Benjamin Graham, has been quoted as saying, "In the short run, the stock market acts as a voting machine, while in the long run, it acts as a weighing machine." What is voted upon are price and profit potential, while what is actually weighed are real profits.

In the short run, people vote their hopes and fears, driving up (or down) the prices of stocks; emotions and market psychology hold sway, so such "voting" is generally based on fear and/or exuberance rather than on fundamentals.

In the long term, stocks are a machine that weighs the soundness, stability, profitability, and long-term prospects for the companies they represent. Unfortunately, average stock market investors tend to overlook the long term but rather react to short-term perturbations and, thus, far underperform the market, falling far short of obtaining the potential long-term appreciation from their stock.

Average investors tend to become overly exuberant when their stock is up 10 points but very depressed when it is down 10 points. Watching such price movement just heightens emotions. Over the long haul, real wealth is created by latching onto great businesses that are run by fine, honest managers who act as owners, who make correct asset allocation decisions, and who grow their dividends and value of their business over a long period of time. **Or, as John Bogle, author and founder of Vanguard financial services, observes, "Time is your friend, impulse is your enemy."**

A study done by David Dreman from 1985 to 2006 focused on the chances of having a loss from stock investing.[6] It looked at different time periods—one year, two years, three years, all the way to 10 years—and found that the chances of having a loss in a day trade—the purchase and sale of the same security on the same day—is about 50 percent. I don't know about you, but a 50 percent chance of loss isn't very attractive to me. But when you move out to holding that stock for three years, the chance of it becoming a loss drops to about 14 percent. That's a significant difference over a day trader who has 50-50 odds. And if you move all the way out to 10 years, there's nearly zero percent chance of loss.

The Dreman study also looked at the broad market

---

6 David Dreman, *Contrarian Investment Strategies for the Next Generation* (New York: Simon & Schuster, 1998).

but failed to consider well-run companies vs. less solid enterprises. If you couple the longer term holding period with due diligence and research and you are buying well-managed businesses and hold them for a longer term, then your odds of loss go down even more.

A key to being a successful investor is to develop the ability to block out the emotional roller coaster of short-term volatility and focus on the more important long-term fundamentals.

15: Emotion Can Be the Enemy

Many times, investors can be their own worst enemy. They tend to act in concert, following a "herd" mentality rather than thinking independently or in the contrarian manner discussed earlier.

Depending on conditions, investors either worry about the market taking off without them or, if the market drops, whether they should sell everything. Such "emotional investing" can be likened to riding an elephant. The emotional part of your brain is the elephant, and the rational part is you on the elephant's back. When things are going fine, you feel like you're in control. However, when the elephant gets scared, all you can do is hold on. The emotional side of the brain takes over and shuts off most, if not all, of the rational part.

Obviously giving into emotion will not help with investing. But you can take certain steps to "ride the elephant":

1. Recognize the problem and try to put it in perspective. Is it as bad as it really seems, or are you giving into herd mentality?

2. Identify the source of the stress. What is the trigger? Is it something at home, on the job, or a financial situation? Difficulties in any of these areas can cause stress, but you have control over how much emphasis to put on them. Sometimes people think that these areas define them, but the truth is, as human beings, we are much more than any material wealth or possession.

3. Allow yourself to grieve. It's OK to recognize that things didn't work out the way you anticipated.

4. Anticipate the worst-case scenario. Facing fears head-on helps reduce stress and encourages logical decision-making.

5. Recognize that the market will change. Nothing goes up forever, nor does it always stay down.

And the truth is, things are rarely as good or as bad as they seem. In a study done by Dalbar and Associates from 1984 to 2001, the S&P 500 (see box) generated an average return of 16.3 percent per year (including dividends), while the average equity fund investor realized average returns of just 5.3 percent per year.

S & P 500: A Race to Wealth

The Standard & Poors 500 (S&P 500) has been widely regarded as the best single gauge of the large-cap U.S. equities market since the index was first published in 1957. The index has over \$3.5 trillion benchmarked with index assets comprising approximately \$915 billion of this total. The index includes the 500 leading U.S. companies that capture 75 percent of this country's equities. The S&P 500 is considered to be the bellwether and primary indicator of future trends in the U.S. economy.

Source: www.standardandpoors.com

During the greatest bull market in history, the average individual investor realized only about a third of the total broad equity market performance! According to Dalbar, this was primarily due to buying and selling at the wrong time.

During broad market rallies, confidence in equities rose and investors bought more stocks at higher prices. When the market experienced strong declines, fear increased, and investors then sold in a panic at lower prices. Emotion and broad market psychology held sway. Rather than basing decisions on economic or company fundamentals, in both scenarios, investors gave into excessive exuberance or fear.

By following a more disciplined, fundamentals-based tactical investing strategy and using a properly diversified portfolio allocation, you can reduce emotional reactions and improve long-term results.

16: *Avoid Large Losses*

Warren Buffett is credited with the wise saying: "Rule Number One in investing is to not lose money. Rule Number Two is to remember Rule Number One." It is of course virtually impossible to never lose money investing, and even Warren Buffett has experienced losses on many occasions. He is making reference to the fact that every investor's goal should be to avoid large or unrecoverable losses.

Large losses can devastate your investment portfolio. For example, if your portfolio declines 10-15 percent over a certain time period, it is certainly not pleasant, but with a rebound of 13-28 percent, you can be back to where you started. But if your portfolio suffers a drop of 25 percent, 40 percent, or more, it would require a rebound of 50-80 percent just to reclaim the original figure!

This same math applies to other types of investments. How long will it take those high-flying tech stocks to recover from their dramatic declines? Will they ever again see those outrageous valuations? I seriously doubt it! Or what about your house—how long will it be before it recovers the 25 percent drop in market value since the peak in 2006? Obviously, sometimes these declines are unavoidable (though I guess we all could have sold our houses in 2007 and rented, but then who would have bought?) But when you can, take every precaution to avoid the life-changing consequences of a severe decline in portfolio value.

For the most part, avoid the arbitrary use of stop-loss orders in your equity accounts as a way to limit losses (see box). The judicious use of such trading tools might be appropriate for more volatile holdings but not for stocks that you consider to be high quality or core. If anything, you might want to buy more of a great business if it is put on sale in a volatile market. If a business is great—as discussed earlier and in upcoming chapters—it can help investors avoid large declines in stock prices and help support the valuation level of the company's shares over time.

When Is Enough Loss Enough?

Designed to limit an investor's loss, a stop-loss order is placed to sell a security when it reaches a certain price. For example, setting a stop-loss order for 10 percent below the price you paid for the stock will potentially limit your loss to 10 percent. This strategy allows investors to determine their loss limit in advance and helps prevent emotional decision-making.

Source: www.investopedia.com

Before moving on to Part 2, "Value Investing Strategy," take time to explore some of the common myths about value investing in the next section.

WISE INVESTING VALUE RULE NO. 2

Stay within your circle of competency, focus on the long term, and control your emotions. These three things can increase your chances of being successful in the long term.

Value Returns

SECTION III:

Myths of Value Investing

17: Value Doesn't Grow

A common myth is that value stocks fail to grow; this is based, in part, on the terms growth and value. The word growth directly implies that a stock's value will increase. As a result, using value as compared to growth makes it sound like value stocks don't grow. In addition, investing for growth is also compared to investing for income. Thus, it seems plausible to follow the growth-style path instead of investing in stodgy old value stocks. Such thinking, however, is completely illogical.

Value investing has been defined as paying a reasonable price today for a future stream of earnings. It stands to reason that the value stock that you're buying is expected to produce future earnings, or you wouldn't buy it. It makes no sense to say that value stocks don't grow their earnings or dividends. They do. Many of these value stocks are growing at a much faster pace than traditional growth stocks, but they trade at much more reasonable valuations, so you're taking less risk in buying them. Such value stocks could almost be called growth stocks in disguise!

18: Value Investing Is Complicated

Another myth is that value investing is complicated. Well, if successful investing was easy, everybody could do it, and we'd all be rich. To be good at any type of investing, whether it involves fundamental analysis of companies, technical charting of stocks, or knowing when to buy or sell a piece of property, involves a certain amount of study and quite a bit of work.

For that matter, being good at almost anything requires effort and discipline. Professional athletes did not achieve incredible success by simply being born talented; reaching the top of their game took years of work, discipline, mistakes, and then, finally, triumph. Only rarely do we see or know about the drudgery and errors. **As athletic superstar Michael Jordan has observed, "The minute you get away from the fundamentals—whether it's proper technique, work ethic, or mental preparation—the bottom can fall out of your game, your school work, your job, whatever you're doing."**

Becoming a good value investor requires the ability to read and understand both a company's Value Line and annual reports as part of examining and analyzing its fundamentals, including but not limited to the following:

- How does the company work?
- How does it make money?
- What is the quality of management?
- Are they operating in growing markets?

There is work involved just as with any worthwhile activity. Again, if it was easy, everyone could do it.

People who don't take the time to really learn about investing do so to their own detriment. Unless you inherited a lot of money—or even if you did and plan on spending it—you'll need to learn how to manage or invest your money or at least find a professional who can efficiently and honestly do it for you.

Whatever you do, avoid taking shortcuts, such as looking at a chart or listening to "get-rich-quick" pundits. This is what the average person does, and they are not becoming wealthy, so why copy them? Instead, find somebody who understands how to invest successfully and let them help you. After all, this is your lifestyle, retirement, and family's future. It's worth taking the time to become a competent investor or to understand enough about investment to seek help from a qualified expert.

19: Value Investors Don't Sell

Another myth is that value investors never sell. It seems that their mantra is "Buy and hold; buy and hold." While it's true that most value investors are less trading-oriented than growth stock investors, even the greatest value investor, Warren Buffett, sells when he determines that his investment in a particular company no longer provides a better return than he could get from a comparable investment somewhere else.

Value investors sell less often because exceptional companies are difficult to find. They continue to own their shares as long as they are producing future earnings growth relative to their price that is attractive to the investment. There's nothing wrong with selling a portion of the shares of a great company when it's fully valued or overvalued, especially if you think there are better opportunities elsewhere. But given how hard it is to find a good investment, why sell just to get a quick gain; where else will you put your money?

At times, value investors will buy a stock as a trade, fix a target price when they think it's going to be fully valued, and sell it when it reaches that target price. However, in this case, a trade usually does not mean later that day or week but rather several months down the road. In the short run, it is almost impossible to predict what the market will do, so buying a stock with the idea that it should be traded a few days later ignores the market's natural volatility.

20: *Value Investments Are Just Cheap Stocks*

Yet another common myth is that value stocks are just inexpensive stocks. The thinking here is that it's gone down a large amount, so now it must be a good deal. Just because a stock was trading at $80 five years ago and is now at $20 doesn't make it inexpensive or a good value. Such thinking is known as anchoring; you're anchoring your value assessment to that higher price, so anything lower begins to seem like a bargain. But who is to say that that $80 was the right price; it might have been abnormally high. Thus, you have to analyze the $80 relative to something else to determine whether it's a good value. The most common metric to determine valuation is the price relative to its earnings (P/E) using the P/E ratio [see box].

P /E: Vital Statistics

A P/E ratio is calculated by dividing the share price by earnings per share (EPS). For example, a company trading at $10 per share that earned $1 per share in a year has a P/E of 10 for that year. Generally, the higher a company's P/E ratio, the more investors expect stronger earnings growth in the future. However, investment decisions should never be solely based on a company's P/E ratio. It is merely a starting point leading investors to inexpensive but good sectors and stocks that could possibly meet the criteria for a successful value investment.

Cheap stocks are not necessarily value stocks. Value stocks not only refer to the price but also the price relative to what an investor will get in future earnings from the company.

WISE INVESTING VALUE RULE NO. 3

There is a reason why some so-called "rules" are really myths. Think for yourself, and do your own homework.

PART 2:
VALUE INVESTING STRATEGY

Value Returns

SECTION I:

Tactical Value Investing

21: The Old Way—Buy and Hold

During the previous secular bull market of 1982-2000, we used the buy-and-hold strategy for most equity investing. Basically buy and hold involved the process of buying shares of companies after extensive research, such as looking at their fundamentals and determining whether they met our criteria for well-run businesses. Among other things, criteria included determining whether the companies generated consistent and predictable free cash flow and had strong balance sheets (see box).

Getting the Number on Free Cash Flow

One basic way to calculate free cash flow (FCF): Net Income + Depreciation/Amortization – Capital Expenditures = FCF

Earnings can be manipulated or massaged due to accounting gimmicks, but it's much harder for a company to misrepresent its free cash flow. Free cash flow, in many instances, is a better indicator of a company's financial health.

Once we determined that the quality of the business was good, we then established the price that would allow us to buy into it at an attractive valuation. In other words, we did our homework—we knew what we were buying, why we wanted to buy it, and how much we wanted to pay for it.

Our ownership of these shares represented a "real-life" interest and investment in an operating company—not just pieces of paper to be shuffled around like playing cards.

Also, rather than setting a "sell-by" price—once the stock reached a certain dollar value, it would be sold—we mostly focused on the long-term growth of earnings and dividends that would to be reflected in a consistently increasing stock price over time.

What would be the point of putting hard work into finding, analyzing, and buying stocks only to turn right around and sell them a short time later at a 15-20 percent profit? We would potentially miss out on the long-term appreciation that might allow us to double (or more) our investment over an 8-10 year time horizon.

Investing in shares of quality companies during the secular bull market of 1982-2000 was enjoyable, profitable, and interesting with a minimum of time and energy required to figure out where to sell them or how the overall economic environment might impact their future growth.

22: The New Reality—Tactical Value Investing

But those days ended when the equity market peaked in 2000, and it may be as long as another 5-10 years before the economic fundamentals align to form the basis for a new secular bull market.

In the current overall financial environment, exclusively using a buy-and-hold strategy for investing is counterproductive in achieving your long-term financial goals. The reasons for this will be explained in more detail in upcoming chapters, but briefly, the reality is that corporate earnings will not grow as quickly or as consistently, translating into flat or declining price-to-earnings (P/E) levels in the market. This equals long-term stagnation in stock prices with increased short-term volatility.

Hence, simply buying and holding equities is far less profitable today. You still need to put in the time and effort to locate and analyze promising companies for purchase to determine whether they meet the requirements for soundness and high quality, but another layer of complexity has been added. In addition to determining the price level at which the companies would be a desirable purchase, you also need to figure out the proper valuation level that represents full price or over-valuation that might indicate the need to reduce the position size or sell outright.

For many individual investors, the process of determining when to buy and sell can be the most challenging facet of equity investing, but to ignore the criteria is to open the door to increased risk and mediocrity in investment performance.

Therefore, the type of value investing we practice today is known as a tactical value strategy. This method still includes the more traditional approach of buying great businesses with solid free cash flow and growing dividends while being careful to buy when they're on sale and holding them for longer term appreciation. But to supplement this, we also purchase solid, well-run businesses as tactical value trades. Such businesses operate on a cyclical basis or have short-term hurdles that temporarily impair their growth. For example, the earnings of energy companies tend to be cyclical in nature and their stocks fluctuate significantly with changes in oil prices. These elements, however, can make them useful trading candidates. Tactical value strategy represents a necessary transition from the buy-and-hold strategy, which will be discussed in greater detail later in the book.

The first step in implementing either strategy, however, is to do a fundamental analysis of individual equities. This requires examining several criteria. The next section discusses characteristics and long-term core elements to look for in companies, including those purchased for a limited period as a trade.

WISE INVESTING VALUE RULE NO. 4

To everything there is a season. Buy and hold alone worked in the last secular bull, but in the current secular bear, you also have to include a more active component to your portfolio.

Value Returns

SECTION II:

Qualities of Exceptional Companies

23: First Class Management

Does a company have first class management?

Often overlooked by the average investor, this question can be difficult to answer and is intangible in some respects, but it's also extremely important; in many cases, quality companies with a good market share, products, and services have been killed by bad management.

So how do you determine whether a company has good management? Such information is rarely found by following the latest media and water-cooler speculation, reading a magazine article, or even using the Value Line investment research tool (www.valueline.com), which provides a snapshot of about 15 years of company history. While Value Line can be a good starting point, the real answer is found in several years' worth of the company's annual report.

The first thing to look for is the chairperson's letter, usually located up front. In this letter, the CEO often says something like "This is what we did last year; this is why; and this is what we think is going to happen this year." What should jump out is the question of are they being straightforward or are they talking around the issues? The latter is usually a red flag. Look for a CEO who lays it on the line and admits if they messed up. Conversely, if management did a good job, they should say so, giving credit where credit is due. Of course, there's no way of telling if such recognition is actually deserved, but managers who share the credit (instead of taking it all for themselves) are more likely to be effective and forthright.

You'll also want to see what promises were made over the years and if they were kept. For instance, examine how closely the projected earnings were to what really happened in subsequent years. Top management ought to have a pretty good idea of how well they believe the company will do, and it's a bad sign if they are markedly wrong. For this, you'll need several previous years' worth of annual reports to spot trends that will help you assess management. Another red flag is if a new project, focus, or expansion is mentioned one year and not the next.

Also look for whether key people have been in the company or in the industry for a while. It takes time to get to know a specific market and take advantage of the opportunities to maximize that company's potential. Many companies and industries have steep learning curves, so high turnover among key players is another warning sign. Adversity is a good teacher, and it helps if management has been through both good and bad markets as well as business cycles within that industry.

24: A Stake in Ownership

Does the company's management have a significant ownership stake in the business?

It's an axiom of human nature that you care more about what you own than what you don't. Most people take better care of homes they own as opposed to rentals; some mortgage companies refuse to lend to or charge higher interest rates to condo purchasers if a certain percentage of the units are occupied by renters. The same is true of cars and just about everything else that's purchased instead of leased. Similarly, people work harder at their jobs if they own their own business rather than being an employee due both to personal pride and their bottom line.

Hence, if a company's management owns stock in that business, they certainly will have a stake in making sure it does well. Many studies have shown that companies with high insider ownership outperform those with low insider ownership. It makes sense; ownership provides an incentive.

Therefore, it's imperative that managers act like owners, regardless of whether they actually are. They make decisions that have major influence on the success or failure of that company. Key among them are decisions on allocating capital; how money gets invested helps determine the fate of the company and what its long-term returns will be. These capital allocation decisions should be made by an "owner" focused on long-term value creation—not managers with a short-term horizon.

Alternatively, "managers" could instead simply try to make the company bigger. Expanding the company and acquiring assets with the goal of "bigger is better" may not be beneficial to shareholders. In this media-crazed culture, it has become fashionable for investors and the news media to idolize "superstar" chief executives. Unfortunately, some of these CEOs start to believe in their invincibility to the detriment of the company and its shareholders; investors should get worried when CEOs begin to assume they can do whatever they want.

Another thing to watch out for is stock options that allow executives to buy stock in the company at a reduced price during a specified period of time. Option-laden management has a clear conflict of interest. Such options provide an incentive to be aggressive, to have that company's stock price increase by any means necessary, so they can sell their options and then take the cash. Stock options also provide great personal incentives to do potentially unwise things, such as repurchasing shares when the stock is overvalued or engaging in phony accounting practices, as with Enron in 2001, resulting in the company's bankruptcy. In such cases, the goal is to only increase the price in the short run. On the other hand, if these short-term moves backfire and the stock price goes down, these managers lose a minimal amount of money; they simply lose out on potential profits. For such managers, stock options are a way of saying "heads, I win big; tails, I walk away virtually unscathed."

25: *Solid Return on Capital*

Does the company generate high returns on invested capital?

Something near and dear to any investor's heart is finding a company that generates high returns on their invested capital; these high returns ultimately translate into a growing stock price. To find such companies, investors should look at both a company's return on equity and its return on capital. Return on equity (ROE) measures a corporation's profitability by revealing how much profit a company generates with the money shareholders have invested. For example, if a company invests $1 of equity and generates a total return of $1.20, their ROE is 20 percent. ROE statistics, however, can be misleading. A company can report a high ROE if it is highly leveraged with a lot of debt and a small amount of equity. This reported profitability masks the fact that it is taking a great deal of risk to get these high returns on equity.

Return on capital (ROC) measures how effectively a company uses all of the money that's invested in its operations. Compare that statistic to other companies in similar industries as well as other industries. Low ROC means that all the money that is reinvested (not paid out as dividends) is compounding at low rates of return, which is not a favorable prospect for an investor.

To calculate the ROC, divide the net operating income after tax (NOPAT) by the total invested capital (debt and equity). The data can be found in a company's annual report within its financial statements. Here is the formula:

ROC=NOPAT/(Debt + Equity - Cash)

Management is creating value for their shareholders when the return on capital is greater than the company's weighted average cost of capital (WACC). WACC is a calculation of a company's cost of capital, which is proportionately weighted depending on how much a company's assets are financed by either equity or debt. WACC gives management and investors a good look at the overall required return an asset must generate to break even. A company with an ROC below WACC is losing money and failing to create value.

26: *Low-Cost Operations*

Does the company have low-cost operations relative to its competitors?

A low-cost producer can beat out the competition, capture increasing market share, and survive economic downturns. This becomes especially important in a commodity-type business (such as food, utilities, energy, or other natural resources) as opposed to a service-oriented business. As an investor, you want to own the low-cost producers, and this can be found by looking at company's profit margin data, which is available on Value Line investment research (www.valueline.com) as well as in the company's annual report. Also examine the margins over time, which should ideally be increasing relative to both the company's competitors and other companies.

Many commoditized business models with low barriers to entry are also only marginally profitable over time and may make better trades than long-term core investments. Commoditized business models tend to be very price-sensitive with little brand loyalty from customers—for example, a gas station that must compete largely on just price.

27: Growing Market Share

Does the company have a dominant and/or growing market share in a growing industry?

Both criteria are important; a dominant market share in a static industry is undesirable, as a company needs to have a growing market share in a growing industry. For example, imagine investing in the number one company in buggy whips when the automobile was being developed or in textiles in the United States in the 1990s as the industry was being outsourced to foreign countries.

Hence, look beyond the company and understand what is going on in the general market(s). If the company in question operates in many different markets, take into account what their positions are relative to their competition. Also, find out whether the company is growing its position and profitability in each market.

Having a growing market along with a significant or dominant market share in an expanding industry usually gives a company pricing power, the cash flow to innovate, and the economies of scale to lower their cost of production, so they can continue to develop. In slower economic times, strong companies can increase their market share by acquiring weaker competition. Thus, they come out even stronger.

Some investors make the mistake of only looking for companies that are growing their earnings. However, in order for companies to grow their earnings on a long-term basis, they have to be growing their revenues, as they can only slash costs so much. There are basically two things they can do to grow their revenues—raise their prices or sell more goods. In a low inflation or deflation environment, companies cannot raise their prices very much, or they will lose market share. So, in today's economy, companies can only markedly increase their revenues by growing their market share in a sector that's expanding. They do this by providing a better service or product at the lowest possible cost, acquiring their competition, or—if they are in a rapidly growing industry—providing a good enough product to keep up with demand.

28: *Avoiding Obsolescence*

Does the company provide a product or service that meets current needs?

When you invest in a company, you want to be sure that the company as well as the industry will be around in the future. If the company disappears or if that industry falls into disfavor, the stock price will meet a similar fate. Future earnings can no longer be expected or generated.

One way of measuring a stock's value is to determine the net present value (NPV) of the expected stream of future earnings if all of those earnings were paid out to shareholders instead of being retained by the company. This stream of earnings allows the investor to share in the cash flow that the company generates from its operations. A diminishing or disappearing earnings stream could equate to low or nonexistent stock appreciation.

The following are examples of companies and industries less likely to become obsolete:

- *Railroads*—There will be a continuing need to move heavy, bulky goods long distances. Railroads provide an inexpensive and reliable way to do this.
- *The waste industry*—There is "gold" in garbage. Trash and waste will always be generated, and as developing economies emerge and incomes rise, more and more goods are likely to be built and consumed, adding to the pile.
- *Brand-name food products*—Obviously, we all need high quality food that tastes good, and brand recognition helps guarantee that.

- *Insurance*—People are still going to require insurance, including life, home, and vehicle.

Contrast these industries to the technology area; those companies must continually innovate to stay afloat, and who can predict how successful each "reinvention" will be? In addition, who knows what types of technology will be on the cutting edge? For example, will the current leading semiconductor be state-of-the-art over the next several years? Thanks to rapid, constant advances in technology, what is great today may be completely obsolete tomorrow much less five years from now. Without such knowledge, how can anyone guesstimate what they are going to earn? Notwithstanding, some tech companies with mature business models and strong competitive market positions have evolved into slower growing, value-focused investments that look attractive at current valuations.

29: High Quality Earnings

Does the company have high quality earnings with no accounting irregularities?

One of the big news stories of 2001 was Enron. Suddenly, everyone became aware of the problems that bad accounting practices can cause. Unfortunately, since there are many ways to "cook the books," an astute investor should be aware of what to look out for. Pat Dorsey, at www.morningstar.com, wrote two columns in December 2001 on accounting-related red flags a potential stock purchaser should look for, including the following:

- You want management to run the business and investors to be concerned about the stock prices. Hence, watch out if a firm's management is more interested in promoting the stock than running the business.

- The chief financial officer (CFO) and the corporate auditors should know the books better than anyone else. It's a bad sign if the CFO leaves when the company is already having accounting problems.

- Companies can do a number of things to increase their bottom lines, especially by reporting pension-related gains. In 2000, 12 percent of General Electric's earnings were non-cash income from a credit they received from having an overfunded pension plan; in other words, 12 percent of their earnings were accounting machinations, not actual earnings.

- Another bad sign is when inventories begin rising faster than sales. Sometimes the buildup is just temporary if a new product is to be introduced, but that is usually the exception rather than the rule.

- The stock market rewards companies that are growing, so companies will do what they can to keep increasing their earnings. One way to do this is to loosen customers' credit terms, which temporarily increases their bottom line. You can spot this in some companies by watching the trends in their accounts receivable balance. Does it seem to increase shortly prior to their earnings release and decline shortly afterward?

- The most basic red flag to watch is cash flow. Over time, increases in both net income and in a company's cash flow from operations should be roughly equal. If cash from operations decline as net income increases, this could signal the company is manipulating their reported earnings but not actually producing "real" profits in the form of cash flow.

Still another accounting red flag revolves around stock options, which are usually excluded from the company's expenses. When their true cost is factored in, many company's earnings either would diminish significantly or disappear. Options are a real expense, and a company with many options may have heavily overstated earnings.

30: Free Cash Flow

Does this company generate real earnings/free cash flow?

Probably the most important characteristic of a successful company is free cash flow. If they do not generate real earnings, also called free cash flow, they probably will not be around for long, for this is how solid companies fund their growth. These cash earnings, also called owner earnings, are different than reported earnings. In an earlier chapter, we showed how reported earnings can be manipulated quite easily in the short run.

Cash earnings are derived by adding reported earnings to non-cash charges, such as amortization of goodwill and depreciation, and then subtracting the capital expenditures required to keep a business running at current production levels. Some companies in America that report earnings are really not earning money. You want to own companies that generate real earnings—not accounting earnings.

One way to evaluate management is to look at what they're doing with these cash earnings. They can use that free cash flow to buy other companies, to innovate, to put into research and development (R&D), to pay down debt, to buy back stock, to pay dividends, or a combination of these. All of these actions help buoy and lift stock prices; thus, as an investor, you'll need to identify companies with free cash flow that will create wealth for you on a long-term basis.

You should also be concerned about the company's financial strength. Having minimal debt and strong free cash generation means the company can not only survive economic downturns but can also fund R&D or even buy their weakened competitors.

We would not go so far as to say we only buy companies with a track record of consistent free cash flow growth, but for a company to meet our quality criteria, it would have to be extremely strong in almost all the other characteristics.

31: Reasonable Payout Ratio

If the company pays dividends, what sort of payout ratio does it have?

Dividends are important: the more the better up to a point. However, be careful with high dividends, especially in relationship to the company's earnings. In other words, too high payout ratios, (which are the ratio of the dividends to the earnings), should be viewed with major caution. For example, if a company earns $1 a share and is paying out

80 cents in dividends, then it's got an 80 percent payout ratio. Paying out 80 percent of earnings in the form of a dividend is a poor business practice, as companies need to retain some income to grow on a long-term basis. In many cases, a payout ratio above 60 percent is a red flag, unless it's a business with a great deal of stability in earnings, such as an electric or gas utility that is regulated or a REIT that is required by law to payout a certain percent (see box). These types of businesses can afford to pay out a much greater percentage of their earnings.

The "REIT" Kind of Investment

A REIT (Real Estate Investment Trust) is a corporation or trust that buys and manages shares in a real estate portfolio, direct real estate, or real estate loans. A REIT that buys and manages income properties is known as an equity REIT, while a REIT that purchases mortgage loans is referred to as a mortgage REIT. Often an equity REIT will invest in apartments, retail shopping centers, and commercial office buildings.

Like other companies, a REIT often trades on a major stock exchange, using the pooled capital of many investors to buy assets. In turn, the REIT earns profits for its shareholders through rents and capital gains. Certain tax advantages are offered to a REIT, which are dictated by applicable federal and state laws and procedures. For example, a REIT may bypass corporate income tax if it distributes at least 90 percent of its taxable income to shareholders annually.

Source: http://www.investorglossary.com/reit.htm

In addition, payout ratios above 60 percent means there is a greater chance of a dividend cut. If earnings were to go down, then the company may very well be forced to reduce their dividends. In bad economic times, the dividend, especially if it is based on a high payout ratio, could be lowered; such reductions are extremely hazardous to your investment portfolio. Most of the time, when a company announces a dividend cut, the perception is (usually, quite rightly) that the company is in trouble, and then its stock price plummets.

In addition, a high dividend payout ratio could be a sign that management thinks that it's future growth potential is very low, that it has little reinvestment opportunities, so they might as well pay back the earnings to investors. So, to qualify as a good investment, high dividends should be coupled with growth. A good rule of thumb would be a payout ratio of 25-45 percent.

WISE INVESTING VALUE RULE NO. 5

Stick with quality, and buy businesses when they are on sale. Be prepared to sell when they become overvalued. Believe in the research you've done, and don't let your emotions control your decision.

PART 3:
THE TIMES
HAVE CHANGED

Value Returns

SECTION 1:

Things Are Different

32: *Change Your Mindset*

For many investors, the cyclical bear market from 1973 to 1974 or the period from 1966 to 1982 when the equity market was virtually flat are just footnotes in historical investing textbooks. For most Baby Boomers, the economic cycle of the last twenty years has been friendly with the economy experiencing extended periods of 8-10 years of prosperity and the equity market advancing consistently upward. These periods were broken only briefly by 6-16-month shallow recessions when it paid to "buy the dips" in the equity market since inevitably, recovery would come and stocks would once again rise higher. This Baby Boomer bull market and economic expansion were largely driven by easy credit.

A pattern of credit expansion really started in the late 1960s with the cycle going parabolic thirty years later in the late 1990s. (When we have a parabolic market rise, we see market volatility expanding in the direction of market trend. New high prices are attracting further interest, and that keeps the rally going.) Such phases represented a pattern of declining interest rates and lax credit standards that drove the development of the greatest credit cycle in the history of the United States and most developed economies. Fueled by the globalization of banking and a period of unusually low risk premiums, debt grew rapidly from 2000 on, fueling price appreciation in many types of assets, including residential real estate and equities.

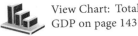 View Chart: Total Credit Market Debt as a Percent of GDP on page 143

The rising asset prices allowed many to enjoy the positive benefits of wealth, driving increased spending on personal consumption and reducing the desire to save. This trend was further underpinned by the increasing number of two-income households reflected by the rise in the Labor Participation Rate from 57 percent in the mid-1970s to a peak of almost 65 percent in 2000. (The Labor Participation Rate is the percentage of working-age persons (typically age 16 to 64) in an economy who are either employed or are unemployed but looking for a job.) However, following the recession in 2001, employment levels never returned to their previous highs and are likely to remain a chronic problem for future economic expansion.

It is our opinion that the same favorable winds that drove the credit expansion and accelerated growth in the economy and equity markets during the last secular cycle shifted beginning in 2000 and are now creating a stiff and formidable headwind. Just as rising employment and asset prices drove up spending, falling or stagnant employment, high debt, and flat or declining asset prices weigh on consumers' ability to spend. Those believing the current economic climate to be a short-lived cyclical recession followed by a return to a lasting recovery and growth in which consumers return to their old free-spending ways are going to be sadly mistaken. They fail to appreciate the magnitude of the deleveraging economy or the underlying issues that have created the conditions leading to chronic high unemployment.

Today, many economists and analysts base their estimates on prior recessions and have made projections of a sharp V-shaped recovery, as had happened in the past. (A "V-shaped recovery" depicts an economic situation where a severe downturn in the economy or markets is met with an equally strong upturn or recovery. The "V" refers to the general shape the downturn and recovery take when shown on a chart.) However, the old data was meaningless since it fell short of the reality that a balance-sheet recession requires years of deleveraging and is inherently deflationary (see box).

Deflation: Less Money, More Bang

The opposite of inflation, which occurs when prices go up, deflation is a decline in general price levels often caused by a reduction in the supply of money or credit. Deflation can also be brought about by direct contractions in spending either in the form of a reduction in government, personal, or investment spending. It also usually has the side effect of increasing unemployment in an economy, since the process often leads to a lower level of demand.

Source: www.investorwords.com

As a result, bank lending drops, savings rates go up, debt gets paid down, interest rates are lowered to almost unheard-of levels, and a deficit spending government runs into limits as to how much it can "stimulate" the economy without destabilizing debt. (When sustained over time, this deficit spending will eventually increase the financial fragility of the economy.)

Bottom line? It is going to be a tough economic and investment environment for probably the next decade. As an investor, you'll need to change how you approach the management of your investment portfolio. It is very important that you develop an understanding of the series of events that lead to the changes in the secular environment and incorporate portfolio strategies that are very different from what worked in the previous economic reality. The next few chapters will hopefully help you do this.

33: Preserve Capital

One of the first things to do when contemplating an investment of your hard-earned money is to determine whether the market is currently in a bull or bear cycle. This is important since the investment strategies that might work well in a bull market could be disastrous in a bear market and vice versa. Your goal is to determine the correct market environment so you can implement the most effective investment strategies.

As of this writing, we are in the midst of a long-term, or secular, bear market cycle, and we might also be entering a shorter term cyclical bear market phase as well. The definition and further explanation of these terms will be discussed more fully in the next section.

During a bear market cycle, strategies placing a greater emphasis on the preservation of investment capital should be favored over those emphasizing the growth of that capital. **As Will Rogers once said, "I am more concerned with the return of my money than the return on my money."** During a bear market, make the safety of your investment capital a primary goal with secondary emphasis on the successful investment of that capital for growth.

This is imperative because the wealth-destroying power of declining valuations in equities during bear markets can erode years of capital gains in mere months. Therefore, chasing stocks with extended valuation multiples based upon the expectation of realizing future hoped-for earnings is an unrealistic and dangerous gamble.

Rather, focus your investigation on company stocks with steady, albeit more slow, growth combined with a history of consistent dividend payments. The compounding benefit of the growth of the dividend will add significantly to your potential total return, especially since many bear markets are accompanied by low levels of inflation. Keep your capital safe, as you cannot grow what you don't have.

34: Reduce Debt

As stated earlier, many of the problems today in the broad-based economy and investment markets are the result of the excessive buildup of debt on consumer balance sheets over several decades, culminating with the disproportionate use of financial leverage during the final years of the real estate boom.

Excessive levels of debt are nothing new. Debt buildup resulted from the construction of canals, turnpikes, and steamship lines in the 1820s and '30s, culminating in the Panic of 1837. A similar situation occurred in the 1860s due to the development of the railroads, which ended with the Panic of 1873. There was also a large buildup of debt beginning with WWI and continuing through the 1920s to finance the expansion of plants, factories, and grids to supply electrical power. Most of us are familiar with the resulting Great Depression through the stories of friends, family, and history books. In each of these cases, debt buildup was primarily a corporate balance-sheet-related issue, but because the assets built with the debt had the ability to produce income, the debt levels could be reduced over time without the need for extensive deleveraging (see box).

It's All About the Leverage

Deleveraging is the unwinding of debt. Companies use leveraging (i.e., borrowing) to accelerate their growth or return; however, when a company is concerned about defaulting on obligations or rampant losses, it can deleverage its balance sheet and sell off debt to lower its overall risk profile. Deleveraging can have serious financial consequences when a company tries to unwind assets that are illiquid—those items that are not easily or readily converted into cash. In such a case, deleveraging may mean selling assets at a relatively steep discount. As a result, deleveraging may lead to downward pressure on security and asset prices as more and more companies and/or individuals unwind their positions.

Source: www.investorglossary.com

The buildup of debt in the United States and many other developed nations over the past twenty years is different in many respects with the potential for a more protracted and painful path to eventual resolution. This buildup of debt has been primarily on the balance sheets of consumers (i.e., credit cards, mortgages, and other types of loans) and has been related to the appreciation of the home as an investment asset. This could have the broad effect of making the economy unstable— destabilizing the economy—as the home is primarily not an income-producing asset with, therefore, less ability to work down the level of debt over time through the production of increased income. So, in order to reduce debt levels related to declining nationwide home values, there will likely be more instances of default given the concurrent weakness in consumer spending levels and economic growth.

Widespread deleveraging by consumers has the potential not only to keep demand levels depressed and economic growth below average for an extended period, it also is inherently deflationary. Though large-scale deleveraging is destabilizing in the short term, in the long term it is the best path out of the current overleveraged condition. The quicker we move forward with the process, the faster we can reach a point to again resume healthy upward growth.

Move forward to reduce your individual debt levels, and if signs of significant deflation appear, do so as quickly as possible. The last thing you want when saddled with debt is a deflationary economy. In a deflationary environment, money increases in value, but it's much harder to come by, making it more difficult to pay off the debt.

35: Separate Core and Trade

As mentioned previously, you need to approach the management of your equity investment portfolio during a bear market differently than in a bull market. During a consistently upwardly trending bull market you can rely more heavily on the expansion of a stock's valuation to provide you with increasing capital appreciation. This allows you to take a more passive approach by holding a larger percentage of the equity allocation in the shares of high quality, core-oriented companies.

The desirable qualities of core stocks were described in detail earlier, but in general, they're profitable, consistently earning great returns on the money (or capital) shareholders have invested. They are also reliable growers, although not at the same rapid pace as a new company. Nevertheless, their earnings are predictable year in and year out, and they typically pay out earnings to shareholders in the form of a dividend. Finally, core companies are also financially healthy. In other words, they take on minimal debt and often generate large amounts of free cash flow (cash flow after capital expenditures). These are the kinds of companies that during a secular bull market environment, you would be comfortable owning in your portfolio even if the equity market were suddenly to close and you couldn't sell your shares for five years or more.

In a bear market cycle however, you do not have the consistency of this valuation expansion to rely on. In fact, the valuation level of equities could easily decline over time. Therefore, you'll need to reduce your allocation to the passive core holding elements and increase the percentage allocated to a more actively managed style. We are not endorsing excessive trading in a portfolio but are merely suggesting that you reallocate away from predominantly passive core holdings to a more balanced core and active allotment of equities.

Use noncore investments for diversification and greater short-term growth potential. For instance, if the core of your portfolio is made up primarily of large-cap stocks, you might want to add some small-cap or international stocks to the noncore portion of your portfolio for diversification.

Noncore holdings are the portion of your equity portfolio meant to be more nimble and flexible. Use this portion to take advantage of shorter term opportunities in cyclical sectors, for example. Once the investing environment has evolved again to a longer term bullish phase, you can revert to a larger allocation of core holdings.

WISE INVESTING VALUE RULE NO. 6

Many factors that served as catalysts for over two decades have turned into headwinds. A shift from McMansions (credit expansion) to McShacks (deleveraging) will alter the investment environment, calling for a more active and prudent approach.

Value Returns

SECTION II:

Secular Market Trends

36: Cycles Are Everywhere

Mark Twain said, "History does not repeat itself, but it does rhyme." So although it may seem tedious at times to study the lessons of the past, it is necessary to develop an understanding of its lessons in order to form the basis for wise decisions in the future. The chapters in this section will help you understand the basic elements of secular market trends necessary in grasping the fundamental principles of investing.

Cycles exist in nearly all facets of life and are generally accepted and taken for granted. Patterns in the change of the seasons, the phases of the moon, the rise and fall of the tides all recur with varying frequency and touch almost every living creature. Some cycles are short term, while others occur over longer time frames and, therefore, seem less noticeable but are present nonetheless.

For there to be a cycle, some condition or situation must recur over a certain period of time. All cycles have a beginning and an end and many have characteristics that repeat with each cycle.

Certain phrases are used to describe economic cycles. The contraction denotes the period when the economy begins to slow down after a phase of sustained growth. The trough, also called the recession, represents the low point of economic growth. The expansion signifies the beginning of economic growth, and the peak is the pinnacle of that growth phase.

 View Chart: Economic Cycles on page 145

37: *Equity and Income Market Cycles*

Fewer people are familiar with the cycles present in the equity and income investment markets, however. Stock market observers have identified what they believe to be scores of cycles, patterns, correlations, and relationships that give birth to a seemingly endless array of market timing systems and trading schemes. Many of these trading systems are supported by well-researched and tested data appearing to have the ability to move in and out of the equity markets at precisely the correct time to generate easy wealth with minimal risk. However, to date, no one has been successful over the long term; otherwise, everyone would be using this system!

At the other end of the spectrum are those who believe the patterns and relationships within the investment markets are so numerous they are merely random coincidences. However, while the implications of these patterns may not be completely understood, they still may contain useful information.

We want to focus on two specific patterns or cycles: the secular bull market and the secular bear market. In this context, the term secular denotes the long term, as these cycles can take over a decade or sometimes even two to complete their phases. Within these long-term secular trends are numerous shorter term cycles (also called bull and bear markets) that can take from one to several years to complete themselves.

The importance of understanding and recognizing these differing investment climates is vital when designing and implementing a portfolio investment strategy.

Understanding the dominant investment climate and the impact of that climate on different investment approaches is essential for positive outcomes with minimal risk.

38: Historical Patterns

Over the last century, the income and equity markets have seen a number of secular trends that appear to be clear in hindsight. The following is a list of four secular cycles in the U.S. government bond market since 1900.

1. The bear market of 1900-1920 brought yields on long-term government bonds up from a low of 3 percent to a peak of 5 percent.
2. The bull market of 1920-1946 drove yields on government bonds from 5 percent down to 2 percent.
3. The second bear market of 1946-1981 pushed government bond yields from the low of 2 percent to a stratospheric level of 14 percent.
4. The second bull market from 1981 to the present day drove government long bond yields from 14 percent down to the most recent low of 3.5 percent.

Similarly, there have been secular bull and bear market trends in the equity market over the last century.

- The bear market of 1900-1920 took the valuation level (or its price to earnings or P/E) of the equity market from 23x to 5x.

- The bull market of 1920-1929 drove the valuation level from 5 to 22.

- The bear market of 1929-1949 brought the valuation level from a high of 22 back down to a low of 9.

- The bull market of 1949-1966 took the valuation from 9 to 23.

- The valuation fell from 23 to 8 in the bear market of 1966-1982.

- The valuation went from 9 to 40 in the bull market of 1982- 2000.

- In the current bear market, which began in 2000, the valuation dropped from 40 to the most recent low of 13.

Summary: Secular Market Trends

Bear Market Trends:

- Declining P/E Levels
- Rising Interest Rates
- Offset Earnings Growth and Leads to Volatile Markets with Low Absolute Total Returns

Bull Market Trends:

- Increasing P/E Levels
- Falling Interest Rates
- Enhanced Earnings Growth and
- Leads to Trending Markets with High Absolute Total Returns

39: Macro Drivers

Starting in 1900 and ending in 1920, the first equity market cycle in the last century was a bear. It began with the valuation level of the market (P/E) resting at 23, and 20 years later, it was firmly in single digits at 5. Over that 20-year period, the Dow Jones Industrial Average (DJIA) only managed to move from a starting level of 68 to an ending level of 67. However, because within those long-term secular cycles were shorter term cyclical trends as well, the market was far from static. The annual moves in the DJIA during that time swung widely from -38 percent to +82 percent. In fact, though the broad market accomplished little from start to end, 45 percent of the years during this period managed to finish with a positive return in the index.

The really important thing to understand about the drivers of these market trends, however, is that during this secular bear market cycle, the economy continued to grow and corporate earnings rose. These factors are normally positive for equity prices, however during this period they were almost completely offset by a contraction in the valuation level (P/E) of the market.

How did this happen? Certain factors control expected returns from investing in a particular equity and essentially include three elements:

1. The dividend yield and the compounding growth of that dividend
2. The future stream of corporate earnings
3. The market's opinion of the future growth of those earnings, which is expressed in the valuation multiple or P/E ratio

When the market believes that earnings will grow at a faster rate than average, the price of the stock gets bid up as more investors desire to share in the future earnings growth. This produces an expansion in the P/E and can be an explosive driver in stock price appreciation. But when the earnings are expected to be lower than average for a particular company or the market in general, then prices fall as investors become discouraged by future growth prospects, and the P/E contracts. This decline in valuations tends to offset any positive influences from the (slower) earnings and dividend growth.

Looking at the secular historical patterns, at the start of each secular bull market cycle, the market is trading at reasonable valuation levels with single-digit P/E levels. During the secular bull period, the valuation multiples consistently expand, finally peaking with P/E levels typically above 20. During the inevitable secular bear market cycle that follows, valuation levels consistently fell, finally bottoming once again at the single-digit level. This bottoming of valuation levels is the fuel that helps drive the next secular bull phase.

40: *Where Are We Now?*

The next logical question is "Where are we in this historical context right now?" Obviously, only the benefit of hindsight will reveal precisely when the current secular trend will evolve into the next cycle, but some indicators can provide a sense of our approximate location.

Since expansion or contraction of the valuation level of the broad equity market is a hallmark indicator of both secular bull and bear markets, we can determine how the current price-to-earnings (P/E) level of the market fits into the spectrum of previous cycles. This might provide some insight into whether we are closer to the start or the end of the current cycle.

Like most things in life, however, the valuation level of the market isn't quite as straightforward as it probably should be. When looking at earnings and comparing them to price levels, the question is whether it's most accurate and appropriate to use actual or expected future earnings. In most instances, the more optimistic outlook (i.e., a lower P/E) will be found by using future earnings (assuming earnings are growing). Many analysts correctly point out that those earnings expectations may be significantly inaccurate; however, other analysts are just as quick to say that the current equity market level is already discounting those future earnings projections. In our opinion, the most accurate assessment of the P/E of the broad market results from using the sum of the most recent four quarters' historical earnings divided by the current level of the Standard and Poors 500 (S&P 500) index. For example, if the most recent four quarters' historical earnings for the companies in the S&P 500 totaled $80 and the current level of the Index was 1200, then the broad market would be priced at 15 times historical earnings.

As of the this writing, the most recent four quarters' earnings for the S&P 500 equals $79, and the level of the index is 1225. Doing the math gives us a current P/E level for the S&P 500 of 15.5. At the start of this secular bear cycle in 2000, the P/E level of the S&P 500 was at an all time high of 40.

This indicates that while valuation levels are certainly lower than at the start of this secular bear market phase, they haven't yet reached the single digit levels found at the conclusion of previous long-term bear cycles. With previous secular cycles requiring an average of 17-18 years to complete and assuming we are correct in identifying the start of the current secular bear in 2000, then it appears we can expect perhaps another 5 to 7 years of a similar equity market accompanied by a further contraction in valuation levels.

41: *Additional Complications*

This time around, however, the situation is even trickier. Not only are we currently experiencing a garden-variety secular bear market cycle, but it has been complicated by long-term structural economic headwinds.

The U.S. consumer spent much of the last twenty years amassing a huge quantity of debt. Spurred on by the belief that their stock portfolios (during the tech stock boom) or their homes (during the residential real estate boom) would provide a source of significant income during retirement, many have spent the last two decades under-saving and over-borrowing to fund a lifestyle of excess consumption. Many of today's aging baby boomers are only now realizing that they have insufficient savings to retire in comfort and can scarcely maintain the debt service on their stable of expensive toys. At the peak in 2007, total consumer debt service payments were in excess of 130 percent of disposable net income. Through a process of intentional deleveraging and unintentional default, the level has fallen to 120 percent currently but still remains significantly above long-term averages and is certainly destined to decline further.

 View Chart: Household DTI Ratio: Debt vs. Disposable Income on page 147.

Scholarly research shows that excessive debt levels in society lead to extended economic deterioration. Prolonged deleveraging produces vast amounts of unused factory capacity, excess office space, persistently high unemployment, increased systemic financial risk, and, often, periods of deflation. Just like the housing market must clear its unsold stock of inventory before prices can recover, the U.S. economy must work through this redundant capital stock before lasting recovery can become a reality.

Adding to these economic risks is the fact that the average age is increasing, as baby boomers close in on retirement. Most research shows that as people complete their working years, their need for increased income from their investments surpasses their desire for future growth in those assets. Therefore, rather than putting their funds in equity investments, they fund income-oriented options, resulting in a continuing pattern that might delay or hamper the evolution into the next bull market.

 View Chart: United States: Median Age of Baby Boomers During Past Recessions on page 149.

How all of these complications will affect the development and eventual maturation of the current secular cycle remains unknown. What seems certain, however, is that Americans will almost surely save more, spend in closer proportion to their income, and increase their borrowing more slowly or possibly even decrease it outright in the coming years. This will likely translate into slower overall domestic economic growth and could possibly extend the secular cycle beyond its natural transition to the next phase. Patience is the key, but investors should diligently watch for signals that changes are indeed taking place.

42: *What's the Most Likely Outcome?*

The American consumer has played an increasingly large role in global economic growth over the last decade, as spending on goods, services, and housing has driven the expansion of gross domestic product (GDP) growth through the purchase of exports from emerging economies. The total market value of all final goods and services produced in a country in a given year, GDP is equal to total consumer, investment, and government spending plus the value of exports minus the value of imports.[7]

 View Chart: U.S. Consumer in Perspective on page 151.

A newly frugal American consumer most likely means a more subdued growth rate globally, as no other country has such a large and wealthy consumer base. In view of the high debt burden still in many American households and the potential for persistently high unemployment, a protracted years-long period of painful global adjustment appears likely.

 View Chart: U.S. Unemployment Rate on page 153.

Can we avoid or shorten the length of such a growth-inhibiting period of consumer balance sheet adjustment? It's possible, but such an outcome would require significant changes in American consumer behavior as well as global economic policies. Although American consumers should continue to reduce their level of debt and increase savings,

---

7 http://www.investorwords.com

other countries should also encourage and stimulate domestic spending and reduce their large trade surpluses.

The International Monetary Fund (IMF) and other economists have suggested several scenarios for the world economy over the next few years. They range from a very positive outcome—a cooperative effort among international trade partners to restructure key economic imbalances— to a dire picture in which individual countries retreat into protectionist policies leading to a new global recession.

It would be wonderful if all countries would see the benefit of cooperating together to pull back from the brink of financial collapse. However, such an effort would require politically difficult decisions involving trade policies and is probably overly optimistic. Such an outcome seems unlikely unless leaders are pressed by the immediate threat of economic or political turmoil.

Once fear of global financial upheaval becomes a fading memory, each country will likely continue down the same path that led us to this point in the first place, continuing to pursue the policies that best suit its own domestic economic and political objectives. Little thought will be given to the effect those policies will have on the global balance of finance and trade.

With the benefit of hindsight, it is easy to say each of us should have seen the current financial crisis coming. But though some financial experts, including the authors, pointed out the growing imbalances, few expected the swift, severe downturn that occurred. So far, most countries have instituted "Band-Aid" type short-term solutions— essentially "kicking the can" down the road—but little has been done to address the underlying causes of the meltdown or to change the likely future outcomes. Unless coordinated global action is taken to alter the imbalances, we could soon find ourselves once again teetering at the edge of financial disaster.

WISE INVESTING VALUE RULE NO. 7

Cycles exist not only in everyday life but also in economic and investing environments. Understanding market cycles can help you make wise decisions in the future.

Value Returns

PART 4:
HOW TO
INVEST NOW

Value Returns

SECTION I:

Diversification and Allocation

43: You Need a Plan

Even when the overall equity market is rising, you'll need a financial plan that incorporates your future goals, income needs, life expectancy, risk tolerances, and other factors (see box). Developing such a road map—which was discussed in an earlier chapter—is especially important for the long term, as there may be significant periods of time when it may be difficult to achieve short-term financial goals.

Since the tech bubble burst in 2000, many investors have not been able to achieve their desired level of returns even if they used longer term historical averages as their guide rather than the remarkable returns of the 1990s.

The traditional approach in allocating portfolio assets when constructing a financial plan has been to passively and strategically distribute money across equity and income classes while incorporating a system of regular or periodic rebalancing. In today's secular bear market, however, because the portfolio could be exhausted due to an extended period of flat or negative returns, more active management is necessary.

The following chapters will present some viable active management strategies that can potentially help generate improved returns during an environment of declining price-to-earnings (P/E) ratios and flat-to-falling equity prices.

10 Myths of Financial Planning

10. I don't have enough money to warrant developing my financial plan.

9. I have so much money that I don't need a financial plan.

8. What's a financial planner going to tell me that I don't already know?

7. I save into my 401(k) plan every paycheck. That's my plan.

6. Because I expect to get a pension, I can take wild risks with the rest of my money.

5. I just developed a financial plan myself with an online calculator and am satisfied with it.

4. I don't need a financial planner to tell me to save more.

3. Understanding Swahili is easier than understanding my financial plan.

2. I want to work forever anyway, so I don't need a financial plan.

1. This is why I had kids. My kids are my retirement plan.

Source: Gregory S. Smith, CFP®, ChFC®, Managing Director, PWM Head Financial Planner, Wise Investor Group, Robert W. Baird & Co.

44: Broader Diversification, Less Allocation to Equities

Each asset should have good individual returns and a low correlation with other assets to compensate for variations within a particular market. The basic elements of a traditional asset allocation strategy are normally comprised of domestic equity and income assets but sometimes also include foreign equities or income and the occasional addition of commodities, such as food, grains, or metals. If the asset allocation is selected wisely and chosen in the correct proportion, the combined portfolio can achieve a greater compound return with less risk than individual assets on their own.

The process of proper asset allocation has become more difficult because the investment climate of the last two years has been marked by rising correlations between asset classes and extraordinary volatility in financial and monetary systems. During the recent financial turmoil, traditional diversification by geography or asset class provided no cushion, as essentially all "risk-based" assets were simultaneously sold off. This posed significant challenges for conservative investors as some of the basic relationships between asset classes were changed or broken down.

While increased correlation effects have lessened a bit in the last few months, continuing heightened volatility indicates that some instability still remains. This presents investors with essentially two choices: stick with their long-term strategic asset allocation in the hope that the environment will soon return to normal or develop a shorter term tactical asset allocation that reduces levels of portfolio risk and volatility.

In practice, the execution of an asset allocation strategy can be subjective and complex. Researchers have attempted to create models or algorithms that rely on indicators to calculate an optimum asset allocation. This sort of quantitative approach falls short, however, since the assumptions that comprise the model simply can't fit every potential set of economic outcomes. The successful implementation of an asset allocation for an investment portfolio is both an art and a science. It requires equal measures of analysis coupled with intuition and basic common sense. Most important of all, investors must clearly understand their tolerance for risk and volatility. Otherwise, they cannot maintain the allocation plan.

For our clients, we typically develop an individualized strategic asset allocation designed to help them achieve their long-term goals of portfolio growth with minimal risk. However, during unusual periods of economic or financial turmoil (such as 2008-2009), we shifted the portfolio allocation to a more tactical short-term mixture designed to emphasize the reduction of volatility and preservation of capital.

 View Tables: General Asset Allocation Suggestion on pages 155 & 157.

It is important to acknowledge the prolonged periods of volatile sideways movement in equities during a secular bear market. Understanding this will enable the tactical allocation of reducing domestic equities in favor of a more broadly diversified mixture that includes inflation protection, currency hedges, and increased foreign exposure.

45: Hedges Are "Golden"

The inclusion of gold into portfolio allocation is especially important during a secular bear market. Studies have shown that when domestic equities are suffering, gold enjoys the benefits of its own secular bull market. This non-correlation is a chief advantage of including gold in the portfolio.

 View Chart: Gold During Equity Secular Bull and Bear Markets on page 159. Correlation with Gold on page 161.

The traditional strategic allocation model incorporates equity securities as the primary asset class with the objective of capital growth, while the objective of income securities is capital preservation. The inclusion of gold provides a third element to the portfolio—insurance against financial crisis and other "black swans".

Historically, gold prices seem to appreciate long term when interest rates are on the decline. This is due to a connection between the absolute price level of gold, interest rates, and the price of gold relative to all other assets, as pointed out in a 1988 paper co-authored by Lawrence Summers on Gibson's Paradox (see box). The paper concluded that "secular increases in the demand for gold, caused by rising income levels, tend to create an upward draft in the real price of gold; that is, secular deflation."[8] Secular deflation tends to lower interest rates, which reinforces the rising demand for gold. Essentially, the price of gold and level of interest rates tend to move in opposite directions.

 View Chart: Gold vs. Interest Rates on page 163.

Gibson's Paradox: A Golden Mean

An economic observation made by J. M. Keynes about the correlation between interest rates and general price levels, "Gibson's Paradox," which Keynes discusses in *A Treatise on Money* (1930), was considered a contradiction because it ran

---

8 S T. Robert, B. Barsky, L. H. Summers, "Gibson's Paradox and the Gold Standard." *The Journal of Political Economy* 96:3 (June, 1988): 528-50.

against the general belief that interest rates were correlated to the rate of inflation. Instead, Keynes found that interest rates were highly correlated to wholesale prices but had little to do with the rate of inflation. In this paradox, interest rate movements are connected to the level of prices as opposed to the rate of change in prices.

Source: www.investopedia.com

Still, investing in gold also carries some risks. A major drawback is that it fails to provide income and is, therefore, more advantageous when interest rates are low or falling, thus making the opportunity cost of holding gold versus alternative assets less. And, in the current environment, gold may have moved above its equilibrium price relative to interest rates as a reaction to fears of a financial system collapse, increases in sovereign debt, and sharp currency devaluation. The development and widespread acceptance of exchange listed gold trading vehicles has also increased demand and are likely adding to short-term price movements that could be unsustainable for longer periods of time.

Though it appears that interest rates are likely to remain below long-term historical averages in a very low inflation environment, if rates were to reverse upward, the price of gold could decline. However, as long as we do not enter a prolonged period of rising interest rates, especially if inflation expectations increase, holding gold in a well-diversified portfolio should be beneficial.

46: **Expand International Exposure**

The two most widely watched international economic forecasts, which are published every six months, come from the International Monetary Fund (IMF) and the Organization for Economic Development (OECD). Though the level of global growth they foresee differs slightly, both regard sustained global economic growth as being driven by continued borrowing by governments and consumers of the United States and the United Kingdom.

However, this scenario seems unlikely to become reality. As discussed earlier, the American consumer has reached a point of excessive balance sheet leverage, and the combined losses from the collapse of the tech stock and real estate bubbles has finally resulted in a shift toward savings and away from debt accumulation. America is destined for a more frugal future earmarked by less conspicuous consumption of the latest "toys." This change in consumer attitudes will mean slower growth in the trend of imported goods to the United States, negatively impacting emerging market countries whose economies were built upon the manufacture of goods for the insatiable American consumer.

However, within this change lies opportunity. Once the reality of the newly frugal America is realized, these countries can institute programs of radical and structural reform designed to permanently enhance their consumer spending and domestic demand. For example, China is currently implementing economic policies designed to encourage increased spending by their emerging consumer class. Structural change takes time to implement and even longer to effect, so there is little if any evidence of this in economic statistics released today. But it's the most likely path if it's the country's only realistic option for financial survival.

 View Chart: Global GDP Growth Estimates... Asia is the Leader on page 165.

The corporate sector in developed and emerging countries, such as China, India, and Germany, has come out of the financial crisis in relatively strong shape with solid balance sheets holding prodigious amounts of cash, increased profit margins from effective cost reductions, and peak levels of productivity. U.S. or internationally based companies providing products and services to increasingly affluent consumers in these countries that previously encouraged their citizens to save more and consume less will benefit tremendously as the consumer class grows larger and wealthier over time.

47: Rent the Rallies

During the last secular bear market from 1966 to 1982, there were 17 separate cyclical bull and bear movements in the S&P 500. The average advance in the cyclical bull periods was 38 percent (with a range between 19 and 76 percent), and the average decline in the cyclical bear periods was -25 percent (with a range between -13 and -45 percent). Each market period lasted an average of 18 months.

If an investor had bought a proxy for the S&P 500 at the start of the secular bear market in 1966 and held it passively during the entire 16-year period, ignoring the multitude of cyclical market swings during that span of time, he or she would have achieved virtually zero return from their investment measured from start to finish. If the purchasing power of inflation is taken into account, the investor's portfolio actually declined on an annualized basis.

Therefore, in secular bear markets, the shorter term, countertrend cyclical bull markets are to be rented but not owned. Relying solely on a passive investment style during a secular bear market will almost surely produce poor results. While we are certainly not advocating any form of market timing—a fool's pursuit—it is certainly possible to take advantage of the cyclical market moves within a secular bear by adjusting the overall allocation to equities in the portfolio. You can also add incremental benefits by using an active rotation strategy during various portions of the economic cycle when specific sectors within the broad market have a tendency to outperform.

We will discuss these types of active management portfolio strategies in more detail in the later chapter entitled Tactical Investments.

WISE INVESTING VALUE RULE NO. 8

Achieving financial goals starts with constructing a financial plan. Without one, you don't know how much risk you're taking and how your assets should be invested. During good times, most people put off planning only to make their financial situation more precarious during challenging periods.

SECTION II:

Strategic Investments

48: Why Stick with Core?

Earlier in this book we discussed the qualities of exceptional companies, touching upon owning core stocks in the investment portfolio for the longer term. Following this strategy with a large portion of your equity portfolio is effective during a secular bull market since the rising tide of the upwardly trending market generally expands valuation multiples across the board. Holding a significant portion of your equity portfolio exclusively in these core stocks tends to be less effective in a secular bear market because even though they still may be great businesses, they will not likely appreciate as nicely since P/Es are likely to be flat or contracting.

For many years, the most widely accepted investment strategy for individual stocks or mutual funds was to "buy and hold" them for an extended period. Under this principle you would invest the bulk of your assets in equity-oriented assets and hold them through the interim ups and downs of the market with the promise of long-term growth based upon historical average rates of return. This conviction rests upon the idea of time diversification or the belief that levels of risk decline over longer periods of time.

While research has shown that equity returns are less volatile than bond returns over holding periods of twenty years or more, this is primarily a product of mean reversion; that is, a trend in which a prolonged period of high returns is followed by another long period of low returns. Stock markets alternate between extended periods of bull and bear patterns; one of the primary determinants of return is the price investors are willing to pay for future earnings.

When earnings growth is slower, there is less enthusiasm for the future and less willingness to pay a premium for those earnings. This means less potential for capital appreciation in stock prices from two components: earnings growth and expansion of the valuation multiple.

However, the third component of the total return equation—dividends—and the growth of those dividends become even more important during a secular bear market and are the chief reason that a portion of your equity portfolio should still be invested in stocks of companies with solid business fundamentals and significant competitive advantages, i.e., core stocks.

 View Chart: Core Total Return Stocks vs. S&P 500 on page 167.

49: Invest for Total Return

Stock market returns typically depend on three factors:

1. The level of corporate dividends
2. The rate of corporate earnings
3. What investors are willing to pay for those earnings, which is often measured by price-to-earnings (P/E) ratios

Historically, dividends have typically grown in line with the overall economy, at an annualized rate of about 5 percent each year. Currently, the yield on stocks in the S&P 500 is around 2 percent. Corporate earnings grew at a double-digit pace for several years following the 2001 recession but have declined amid the Great Recession of 2007-2009. U.S. equity prices peaked two months before the recession took hold and proceeded to plunge by roughly 50 percent with exact declines naturally varying by market segment. As prices fell, the 10-year annualized return on equities went negative, prompting much discussion about a "lost decade" for stocks. For investors depending on a constant withdrawal rate to sustain their needs, these lower-than-historical equity returns posed a major challenge.

 View Chart: S&P 500 Dividend Yield on page 169.

Investing a portfolio in income-producing securities, such as high-dividend paying stocks and bonds can potentially generate enough income to meet most investors' needs. But history suggests that the ravages of inflation will eventually eat away at the principal's purchasing power unless the portfolio's principal grows as well.

In contrast, investing for total returns across various asset classes allows for a focus on generating income while also enabling an investor to pursue returns from equities and other asset classes that tend to produce greater long-term returns than fixed income securities. With this approach, income needs can be met by augmenting current yields from dividends and interest with some portion of the portfolio's capital appreciation. We believe this investment approach, characterized by intelligent diversification and opportunistic shifting among asset classes, will prove all the more valuable in the years ahead as this secular bear market continues to unfold.

50: Focus on Dividends

Dividends are an important component of the total return expected from a stock investment in any market environment but become especially critical during a secular bear market due to the slowdown in earnings growth and resultant contraction in the valuation premium paid for future earnings.

Over the longer term, dividend payments and the compounding of those dividends have a material impact on the total return of the equity market. According to Ibbotson, one dollar invested in large company stocks at the start of 1926 with dividends reinvested grew to $2,015 by the end of 2009.[9] This is a compound annual growth rate of 9.6 percent. However, if you take the dividends out of the equation and rely solely on capital appreciation, the very same dollar would only be worth $85. This equals a compound annual growth rate of 5.5 percent.

To further demonstrate the critical impact of dividends on total return, look at the period from 1929 to 1954. During these years, which encompass a secular bear and the start of a secular bull market, the market entered a decline and did not reach its previous high until 25 years later. From August 1929 to October 1954, the equity market experienced no capital appreciation, as it only managed to reach its previous high at the end of the period. However, if dividends are included and reinvested, the total return during the same period was 330 percent.

As can be seen in this example and as already discussed,

9 Ibbotson SBBI, 2010 Classic Yearbook, Market Results for Stocks, Bonds, Bills, and Inflation 1926-2009 (Chicago: Morningstar, 2010)

during secular bear markets, stock prices can extend as long as two decades with little or no appreciation. In such an investing climate, stocks of quality companies with a strong cash flow and a history of increasing their dividends have a significant advantage over non-dividend paying stocks. But you need to more than exclusively focus on companies with only the highest dividend yields. You should also consider the overall fundamental quality of the companies as well.

WISE INVESTING VALUE RULE NO. 9

Dividends have a material impact on the goal of your portfolio and positive total return. Companies paying dividends may not be the most exciting but have slowly and steadily won the race historically.

SECTION III:

Tactical Investments

51: The Portfolio's Nimble Trading Portion

As discussed earlier in the section on tactical value investing, blindly following the long-held Wall Street mantra of exclusively buying and holding equities can lead to disappointing results during secular bear markets. Secular trends can last for years (if not decades) and can be devastating to portfolios unless some portion of the investment portfolio is more actively managed. Within the long-term secular market trend, there are often numerous shorter term cyclical rallies and declines. Recognizing these trends in their early stages can provide an opportunity to increase your equity exposure to benefit from the cyclical advances and reduce it during the cyclical declines. This kind of agility can potentially improve overall portfolio results while limiting risks.

However, this is a complicated process, requiring an understanding of the macroeconomic environment as well as a contrarian bias since to be most effective, you'll need to increase the allocation to equities when the market seems at its weakest point. One of the key benefits of employing a tactical value style is that as the economy and investment climate changes, the sectors providing the best opportunities for good value will alter as well. Using a more nimble approach allows the investor to actively allocate assets into those attractively valued areas.

However, you should avoid market timing—the strategy of buying or selling stocks and other financial assets by attempting to predict future price movements. Constant short-term trading is counterproductive, increases trading costs and taxes, and has yet to be proven to be successful long term. But other techniques can improve your chances of successfully achieving investment goals in a secular bear market. These include using sound analysis based upon fundamental measures of value combined with economic and market cycles to reduce equity exposure at times when the market or specific stocks appear expensive and increasing equity exposure when stocks appear undervalued.

How do you know which portion of the portfolio should be allocated to a more nimble trading strategy versus the traditional core elements to be held for the longer term? The answer is based on individual needs. The proper proportion will be different for each investor and will be based upon such variables as portfolio size, tolerance for higher volatility, time horizon, and even income needs and should be discussed with your investment manager or financial planner.

52: Cyclical Bull Opportunities

Since 2000, we have maintained that the secular bear market shouldn't push conservative investors out of the equity market but instead should be the impetus for a more diligent focus on capital preservation through proper portfolio diversification and utilization of appropriate tactical investment strategies.

However, the level of investment risk fluctuates during the long-term secular trends as shorter term cyclical trends evolve. Near or at the bottom of a cyclical bear market, before the next cyclical bull commences, the level of risk inherent in equity investments generally is less than at or near the peak of the previous cyclical bull. This is because the contraction of P/E levels during the bear market has reduced valuation risk.

The challenge for investors, then, is to identify the variables indicating the change from cyclical bear to bull and vice versa, so they can know when to reduce or increase the level of equity exposure in the portfolio. Several variables can be helpful in making these assessments, including the following:

- Changes in liquidity and the level of interest rates
- Absolute valuation levels of the broad market
- Psychological extremes of the investing public
- The technical position of the market

For example, during the cyclical bottom of the March 2009 market, each of these variables was aligned positively (especially liquidity and rates with the Fed actively participating in the income markets) and indicated a potential change in the short-term direction of equities. Investments in high quality companies, especially those with strong dividends, produced attractive total returns over the following 12 months as the cyclical bull market ran its course.

As discussed earlier, the normal business cycle has four phases: expansion, peak, contraction, and trough. Because the cyclical trends of bull and bear cycles in the equity market tend to be roughly correlated with changes in the economic business cycle, conservative investors should increase their equity allocation near the start of the cyclical bull market and focus more on specific sectors that are likely to perform best in the early portion of the business cycle.

A cyclical bull trend is most likely to emerge near the end of the trough phase but will develop and grow during the expansion and peak phases. During these phases, the sectors most likely to see more pronounced price appreciation are consumer discretionary, materials and industrials, energy, and possibly technology.

53: *Cyclical Bear Risks*

As the economic cycle evolves and by the time the peak phase morphs into the beginning of the contraction phase, the levels of risk in the investment climate have already risen to a point that the conservative investor should begin reducing exposure to the more economically sensitive sectors of the equity market, or they can reallocate those funds into more defensive sectors in anticipation of the contraction and trough phases of the cycle. Very risk-averse investors can put some of the funds into short-term income alternatives.

Cyclical bear markets also develop and continue during contraction and the trough phases of the business cycle. Corporate profits will likely peak and begin to decline, prices of commodities tend to drop, and interest rates begin to move lower. The level of inflation is also most likely to decline, or depending upon the depth of the economic slowdown, disinflation or even outright deflation could develop.

The sectors of the equity market that tend to perform best during the contraction/trough phases during a cyclical bear market are consumer staples, telecom, utilities, health care, and, if short-term interest rates are declining, the financial sector. Also, during these phases the price of corporate and municipal bonds could rise if absolute interest rates decline. Many income securities also have the portfolio diversification benefit of historically being negatively correlated with the equity market, (i.e., their prices tend to move in the opposite direction of the prices of stocks) and can help cushion some volatility in the equity portfolio. Of course, as discussed previously, it is vital to maintain a properly diversified portfolio that includes an appropriate allocation to various securities at any point in the economic cycle.

54: Value of Cash Reserves

There are at least three good reasons for always maintaining a cash position as part of your financial plan but especially during a secular bear market.

Reason No. 1: Liquidity
Apart from day-to-day expenses, typically paid from current cash flow, the need for liquidity generally falls into two categories:

- Emergencies (health problems, job loss, etc.)
- Obligations coming due in the next 1-3 years

Set aside cash equal to 3-6 months of after-tax income for emergency funds. The exact amount that's right for you depends on your job outlook and other sources of income and credit. You should discuss this with your financial planner or advisor.

After that, it's up to you to decide how much to allocate within your portfolio. Your emergency cash reserve may be larger than your portfolio's targeted cash allocation, in which case you'll need to keep at least some cash outside the portfolio. On the other hand, if your portfolio is big enough, you could choose to include your emergency reserve within your targeted cash allocation. Either way, the key is safety and liquidity in case of emergency.

Unlike your emergency reserve, maintained "just in case," also consider cash set aside as "money already spent" to cover known obligations. Known obligations paid from cash reserves can include quarterly estimated income taxes, property taxes, a down payment on a home, your child's wedding, college bills, a vacation, and so on.

Liquidity is extremely important here—don't invest money reserved for short-term obligations in the equity market. Instead, keep it as cash or in highly liquid or shorter-term investments, such as money markets, short-term bonds, CDs, and so forth.

Retirees typically have special liquidity needs. For example, the need for emergency funds may go away—if you're no longer working, there's no need to plan for the possibility of losing your job. However, you may want to set aside enough cash to cover at least 12 months' worth of living expenses.

Beyond that, you should probably keep another 2-4 years' worth of expenses in shorter-term investments as part of the fixed-income portion of your retirement portfolio. That way, when a cyclical bear market comes along, you can avoid having to liquidate other assets during the worst possible time, assuming the bear market lasts only a few years.

Reason No. 2: Flexibility

By holding a percentage of your portfolio in cash, you can take advantage of investment opportunities as they arise. For example, a cash allocation may come in handy if you wish to slightly add or take away equities in your portfolio following the tactical value strategy discussed earlier.

Once again, this means avoiding market timing or even large tactical shifts between stocks, bonds, and cash. The odds against being consistently right are too great to make such a huge bet. However, by shifting your asset allocation 5-10 percent one way or the other, you may be able to add value when you are right without derailing your long-term goals should you make a mistake in judgment.

Reason No. 3: Stability

Bonds have been the traditional choice for reducing a portfolio's overall risk. Bonds tend to perform differently than stocks in the same market conditions—sometimes moving in the opposite direction—a principle called correlation.

Historically, however, cash is even less correlated with stocks. What's more, cash is far less volatile than bonds on average. The big advantage of bonds, of course, is the potential for higher income. That being said, in the appropriate proportion, cash can potentially stabilize your portfolio over time.

Finally, a secular bear market environment may produce an extended period of very low inflation or even outright deflation. In this type of economic climate, the purchasing power of your cash reserve is better preserved.

55: *Know When and How to Sell*

Having managed investment portfolios for many years and having talked to listeners of our radio show and investors during our seminars, we have found that for most people, knowing when and how to sell is the hardest part of the investment process. If this is true of you, you'll need to figure out why you bought the stock in the first place. Once you've done that, you'll get a better idea of when to sell it.

To paraphrase Warren Buffett, buy and sell decisions are linked at the hip. If you've done your research, you'll understand why you want to own this stock. You might be looking for a long-term core holding (i.e., something to hold onto for several years that will hopefully become significantly more valuable). Or maybe you are buying it as a trade because of an anomaly that is causing it to be undervalued at the moment despite the fact that the stock lacks qualities and features that make it desirable for the long term.

If you purchased this stock as a long-term core holding, then the sell decision is really easy. Basically, you don't want to sell it. That's the point of owning a core holding. You know it's a superior company. You've uncovered a gem and want to keep it in your portfolio so the compounding effects of time can work in your favor. If the stock splits and the dividends are reinvested, they will grow over time and may potentially make you wealthy. That's why people search for these great companies.

When it comes down to it, there's only one reason to completely sell a core holding in your portfolio: if something fundamental in the company changes for the worse. It's more than missing earnings for a quarter or two but rather has to do with losing market position, a slowdown or complete stop of free cash flow generation, or management changes that negatively affect the overall quality of the product or service. These big changes are going to affect the long-term growth of that stock in your portfolio.

Whenever you buy core holdings, you have to watch and stay on top of them. Great companies did not become that way over night, nor do they fail quickly. It's a process, an evolution, but if you know the business and follow it closely, you'll be able to see those changes taking place. Again, in our opinion, the only reason to sell completely out of a core holding is if the fundamental quality of the company is eroding.

Of course, you can always reduce the size of your core stock position. If the market pushes it to an extreme valuation level relative to its future earnings growth, dividend yield, and potential price/earnings (PE) expansion, then it makes good sense to "take some money off the table" and reduce the amount that you have invested. That's just good risk management.

Bottom line, the sell decision on core stocks is fairly straightforward. For us, the decision to sell completely is based on fundamental deterioration in the underlying business. Then we may also take some off the table if it becomes extremely overpriced. But it's our intention to own it for the long term as long as it's still a great business.

So what about the stocks you buy to trade? When do you sell them? That's a little harder. For the trading-oriented stocks, you'll need to determine when they are going to be fully valued or even overvalued. So how do you do that?

Again, it's connected to the buy decision, basically the reverse of the same research work you did when analyzing the company before making the decision to purchase. If you do the calculations and figure out that the stock is undervalued—whether your benchmark is price to book, price to earnings, or price to cash flow—and you've determined that this company is undervalued, then the reverse of those calculations will tell you when it's fully valued. So, the determination to figure out whether a stock is fully valued or overvalued is the same math in reverse to conclude that it's undervalued.

Once you've made the decision to sell, don't look back, second guess yourself, or play what-if games. Sometimes a stock that has reached your target price and seems fully valued or maybe even overvalued is going to go onto higher levels because of emotional extremes in the market. Bottom line, you have figured out that this is the point where you feel it's fully valued or overvalued, and your risk versus return is higher at this price than if you take that money and put it into a more undervalued stock. Be confident in your choice.

WISE INVESTING VALUE RULE NO. 10

Tactical value investing requires a more nimble approach that involves an overall understanding of business cycles and the macroeconomic climate. Rather than relying on market timing, you'll need to take advantage of equity cycles (buying and selling) based on fundamental analysis.

PART 5:
PUTTING IT ALL
TOGETHER

Value Returns

SECTION I:

Prepare for the Next Secular Bull Market

56: Long-Term Cycles and Investments

We have described how secular bull and bear market cycles impact individual investment portfolios and provided some suggested approaches to portfolio allocation during the current secular bear market.

As the examples in this book have illustrated, these alternating cycles are essentially driven by the transition from unusually high equity market valuation levels to unusually low valuation multiples. The current secular bear market period is following the same pattern. Having begun in 2000 at rich valuation levels, it experienced several shorter term bull and bear periods but saw each successive market decline achieve a lower level of valuation (though not necessarily a lower level of absolute price). Overall, the broad equity market has provided little durable return over the entire period since mid-2000, yet the current level of valuation shows that we have not yet reached the point necessary to complete the transition. Given the fact that we are simultaneously experiencing a protracted consumer deleveraging process, it seems likely that all these factors converge with the historical duration of typical secular bear markets to indicate the likelihood of several more years of sideways, volatile, and generally unrewarding market activity.

We will likely still see a sequence of short-term cyclical market movements of both bull and bear variety that could encompass most of the remaining decade, culminating in an uncomfortable valuation trough. But nothing lasts forever. Eventually we will reach the low level of valuation necessary to complete the transition to the next secular bull market, which will become the platform for an extended period of attractive returns in equities.

57: Will We See the Transition?

Aside from an unusually low market valuation, what other clues signify the end of the current secular bear cycle? Historical levels of certain economic indicators are one possible gauge. Examining the levels of specific economic indicators at the start of the most recent secular bull market in 1982 can provide insight as to how far indicators will need to fall to reach the next secular bull market. The table below illustrates some of those indicators and compares their current levels with where they stood at the start of the 1982 secular cycle. According to the table, we still have quite a distance to travel. But by keeping a watchful eye on these and other indicators, you can get a sense of progress during this long-term transition phase.

 View Chart: Showing the Difference Between Now and When the Last Secular Bull Market Started on page 171.

But we also need to keep tabs on societal and social trends that could provide early indications of impending change. For example, during the final years of the Great Depression there was a dramatic acceleration in aviation and communication technology. Similarly, in the coming years, we could see major advances in energy production or medical and transportation technologies. There is even the possibility of resurgence in the manufacturing industry.

A continued pattern of depreciation in the U.S. dollar could make our exports more attractive; therefore, we could directly benefit from the increased wealth and consumption by emerging market economies.

However, no single indicator or factor will broadcast a signal of the impending shift to the next secular bull cycle. We need to watch a variety of objective and subjective indicators for clues as to the evolution and final culmination of the current secular bear.

58: What to Do When It Happens

Eventually, the current secular bear market will end, and we will see the start of a new secular bull environment. When that does occur, it seems appropriate to utilize strategies that are the reverse of those employed during secular bear markets, which were discussed in the majority of this book. In secular bull markets, the overall trend of the equity market is upward with any setbacks typically being more than compensated for by the subsequent recovery and increase in stock prices. The most recent and most dramatic secular bull market is represented by the period from 1982 to 2000.

Although there were certainly cyclical bear markets within the period, such as the Black Monday crash of October 1987 when stocks suffered the biggest one-day percentage drop in history, the overall trend was such that investors who simply bought and held onto stocks saw a strong positive return.

 View Chart: Last Secular Bull Market on page 173.

You should employ strategies designed to maximize the benefits of the long-term upwardly trending market. These include increasing the overall allocation to equities in the portfolio, being cautious about reducing positions or selling for shorter term gains, lowering the allocation to alternative investment classes and international markets, and focusing research on opportunities for greater future earnings growth since a larger portion of the total return will likely be driven by the expansion of the valuation multiple.

However, we have not yet reached that turning point. By following the suggestions contained in this book and conservatively steering your investment portfolio through the rough seas of the current secular bear market, you'll have a greater opportunity to enjoy the benefits of the calm waters and favorable winds of the next secular bull cycle.

WISE INVESTING VALUE RULE NO. 11

Secular bear markets turn into secular bull markets and vice versa. In order to enjoy the prosperous bull market cycles, you need to be able to successfully weather the turbulent bear markets.

Value Returns

CHARTS AND TABLES

Value Returns

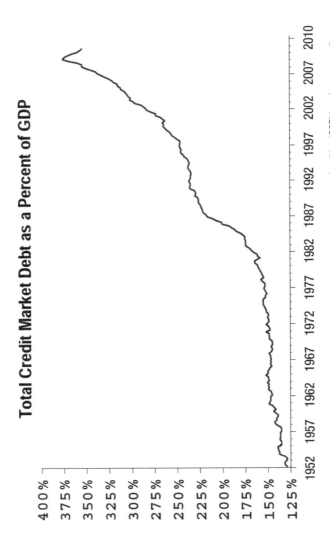

Total Credit Market Debt as a Percent of GDP

1) Chart reflects total credit market debt (households, corporate, financials, government sponsored entities (GSE's) and government) as a percentage of total U.S. GDP. 2) Since 1982, total debt has increased dramatically and though recent trends indicate some reversal, at 350% of GDP we have a long way to go to reach lower historical levels.

Value Returns

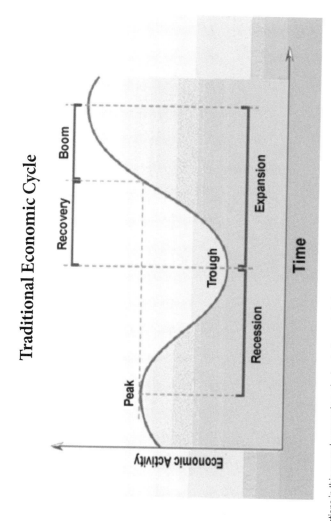

Traditional Economic Cycle

The contractions in this normal economic cycle denote the period where the economy begins to slowdown after a phase of sustained growth. The trough, also called a recession, represents the low point. The expansion signifies the beginning and the peak is the pinnacle. This process repeats itself, but differs in duration.

Value Returns

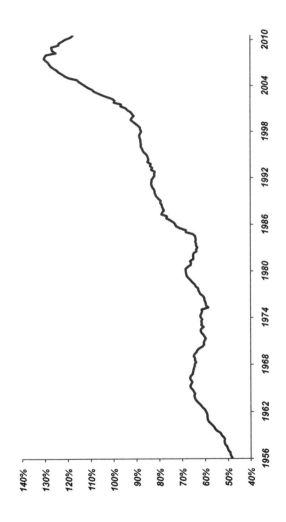

U.S. Household Debt-to-Income

The ratio of outstanding consumer debt to consumer disposable income has more than doubled in the last three decades. Recent declines provide evidence of efforts by consumers to deleverage, either through repayment or default.

Value Returns

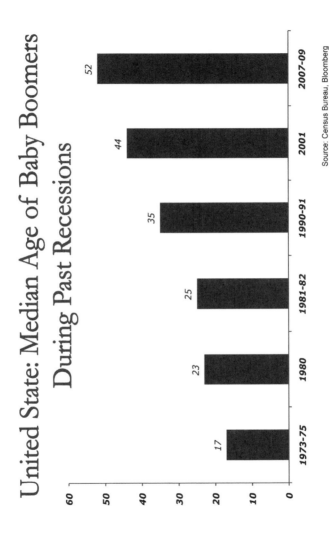

United State: Median Age of Baby Boomers During Past Recessions

1973-75	1980	1981-82	1990-91	2001	2007-09
17	23	25	35	44	52

Source: Census Bureau, Bloomberg

The increase in the median age of baby boomers suggests that their investment risk tolerance and portfolio allocation selections are likely to change as they age.

Value Returns

The U.S. Consumer in Perspective: Percent Share of Global GDP:2009

Country	Percent
United States	16.9%
Japan	8.7%
China	8.6%
Germany	5.7%
France	4.6%
United Kingdom	3.7%
Italy	3.6%
Brazil	2.7%
Spain	2.5%
Canada	2.3%
India	2.3%
Russia	2.1%
Australia	1.6%
Mexico	1.5%
S. Korea	1.4%

Source: Bloomberg

Compared to the current consumption patterns of other countries, US consumers continue to play a large role in global economic growth. As the level of wealth increases in highly populated emerging markets, this dominance by the U.S. could see a marked change.

Value Returns

U.S. U-3 Unemployment Rate

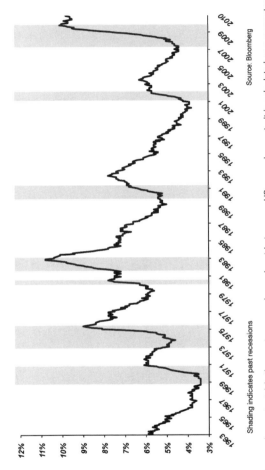

Shading indicates past recessions

Source: Bloomberg

The U-3 (official unemployment rate) is the most commonly used metric to gauge US unemployment. It is calculated as a percentage by dividing the total number of unemployed individuals by the total number of workers making up the labor force. This total does not include those who are employed part-time for economic reasons, discouraged workers who have stopped looking for work or those considered marginally attached to the workforce. This more inclusive definition is known as the U-6 rate and is considerably higher than the official rate.

The allocations are for illustrative purposes only and will not be appropriate for every investor due to individuals' varied time horizons, tolerance for risk and investment needs. Please speak with your financial professional before making any adjustments to your portfolio.

Investments in small- and mid-capitalization companies often are more volatile and face greater risks than investments in larger, more established companies. Foreign investments involve additional risks such as currency rate fluctuations, different and sometimes less strict financial reporting standards and regulation and the potential for political or economic instability. Buying commodities allows for a source of diversification for those who are prepared to assume the risks inherent in the commodities market. Any commodity purchase represents a transaction in a non-income producing asset and is speculative. Therefore, commodities should not represent a significant portion of an individual's portfolio.

General Asset Allocation Suggestions

	Very Conservative Strategic	Moderately Conservative Strategic
General Allocation		
Stocks	40%	55%
Bonds	50%	35%
Cash	10%	10%
Equity Allocation		
Large Cap	70%	50%
Mid/Small Cap	15%	20%
International	10%	15%
Hard Assets	5%	15%

Some general guidelines for asset allocation of the equity, income, and cash portion of your portfolio.

The allocations are for illustrative purposes only and will not be appropriate for every investor due to individuals' varied time horizons, tolerance for risk and investment needs. Please speak with your financial professional before making any adjustments to your portfolio.

Investments in small- and mid-capitalization companies often are more volatile and face greater risks than investments in larger, more established companies. Foreign investments involve additional risks such as currency rate fluctuations, different and sometimes less strict financial reporting standards and regulation and the potential for political or economic instability. Buying commodities allows for a source of diversification for those who are prepared to assume the risks inherent in the commodities market. Any commodity purchase represents a transaction in a non-income producing asset and is speculative. Therefore, commodities should not represent a significant portion of an individual's portfolio.

General Asset Allocation Suggestions

Income Allocation	Very Conservative	Moderately Conservative
Taxable		
1 – 4.99 Years	75%	55%
5 – 14.99 Years	25%	35%
15+ Years	0%	10%
Tax Exempt		
1 – 4.99 Years	30%	20%
5 – 9.99 Years	40%	35%
10 – 14.99 Years	20%	30%
15+ Years	10%	15%

Some general guidelines for asset allocation of the income portion of your portfolio

Value Returns

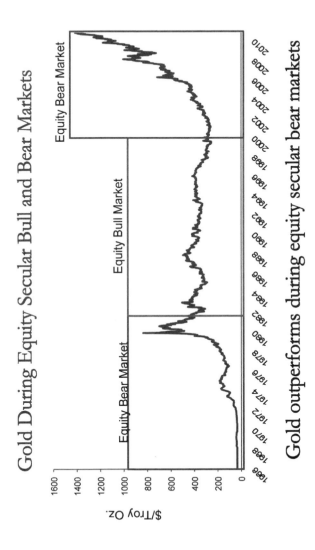

Gold During Equity Secular Bull and Bear Markets

Gold outperforms during equity secular bear markets

Source: Bloomberg

The price of gold performs differently during equity secular bull and bear markets. If the past is any indication, then gold could continue to perform well during the current secular bear market.

Value Returns

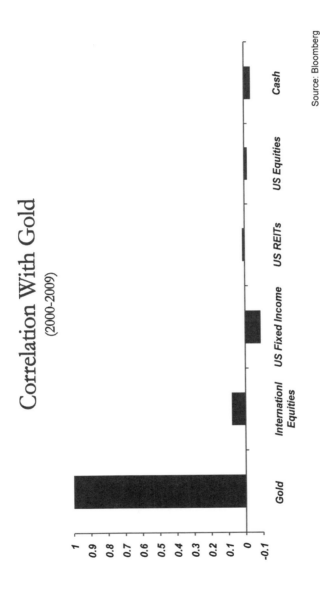

During the last decade, the correlation between gold and other asset classes was practically nonexistent.

Value Returns

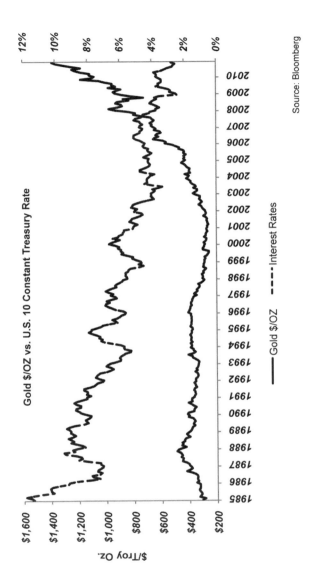

Gold $/OZ vs. U.S. 10 Constant Treasury Rate

—— Gold $/OZ   ----Interest Rates

Source: Bloomberg

Secular deflation leading to lower interest rates tends to reinforce the rising demand for gold.

Value Returns

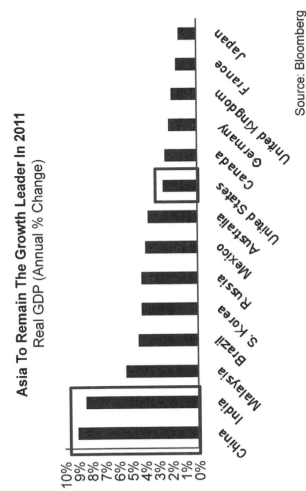

Asia To Remain The Growth Leader In 2011
Real GDP (Annual % Change)

Source: Bloomberg

The future global growth leaders are changing. In the past, the US economy, especially its consumers, were the drivers. Now, more developing economies are emerging due to the implementation of policies designed to encourage increased spending. Investors will need to monitor other economies to gauge future trends in global growth.

Value Returns

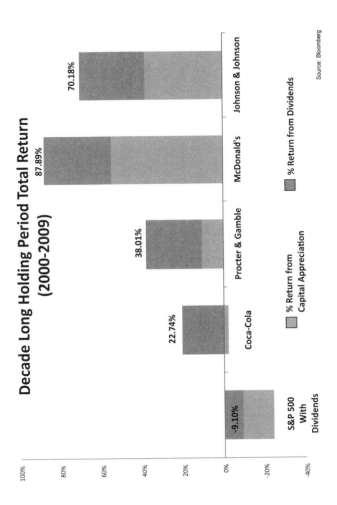

Decade Long Holding Period Total Return (2000-2009)

Source: Bloomberg

Total return is a major factor in growing your assets over the long-term. Even if the price of an asset has remained relatively unchanged, your return may be better than it appears. Dividends and their growth is the chief reason that a portion of an equity portfolio should still be invested in core type stocks.

Value Returns

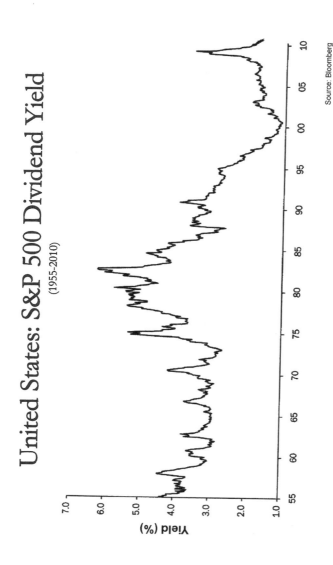

As this historical view of the S&P 500 dividend yield shows, during secular bear markets dividend yields tend to rise, while the opposite occurs during secular bull markets.

Secular Bull Market Economic Data?

Data Point	1Q 1982	Now
Credit Market Data		
Credit Market Debt As % Of GDP	172%	354%
Federal Debt As % of GDP	35%	94%
Household Debt As % Of GDP	47%	96%
Federal Deficit As % of GDP	3.2%	10.6%
Monetary Base	$170 billion and rising	$1.99 trillion and stable to falling
Household Character		
Household Debt Service Ratio	10.7%	12.1%
Mortgage Debt As % OF GDP	31%	76%
Mortgage Debt As % Of D.P.I.	43%	88%
Owners Equity in Real Estate	70%	39%
Personal Savings Rate	11.5%	5.7%
Tax Rates	69% and falling	35% and rising
Unemployment Rate	10.8% and falling	9.8% and rising
Interest Rates And Inflation		
10 Year UST Yield	14.6%	3.5%
Fed Funds	13.2%	0%
Annual Core CPI	8.8%	0.80%
S&P 500 Market Data		
S&P 500 P/E	7.3x's	16.1x's
S&P 500 Dividend Yield	6.7%	1.88%
Misc.		
Global Trade Barriers	High & Falling	Low & Rising

Source: Bloomberg

Certain economic indicators may help indicate the start of the next secular bull market. Their current levels are compared in this table to the start of the last secular bull market (1st quarter 1982).

Value Returns

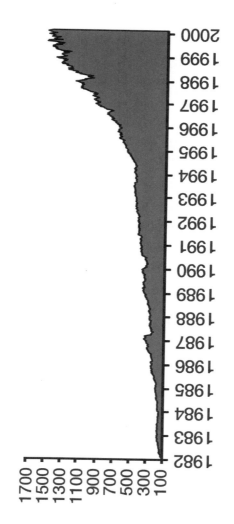

S&P 500 Secular Bull Market
July 1982 – September 2000

Source: Bloomberg

The mindset during secular bull markets is different than one in a bear market. During secular bull markets, the more traditional ways of value investing are applicable and market pullbacks serve as a long term buying opportunity.

Value Returns

FOR FURTHER READING

- Katsenelson, Vitaliy, *Active Value Investing,* Wiley Finance, 2007

- Alexander, Michael, *Investing in a Secular Bear Market,* iUniverse, Inc., 2005

- Easterling, Ed, *Unexpected Returns,* Cypress House, 2005

- Stein, Robert, *The Bull inside the Bear,* John Wiley & Sons, 2009

- Dreman, David, *Contrarian Investment Strategies: The Next Generation,* Simon & Schuster, 1998

- Greenwald, Bruce, *Value Investing from Graham to Buffett and Beyond,* John Wiley & Sons, 2001

- Graham, Benjamin, *The Intelligent Investor,* Harper Business, 1973 (4th Edition)

- Graham, Benjamin, *The Interpretation of Financial Statements,* Harper Business, 1998 (Updated by Michael Price)

- Klarman, Seth, *Margin of Safety: Risk-Averse Value Investing Strategies for the Thoughtful Investor,* Harper Collins, 1991

- Kindleberger, Charles, *Manias, Panics and Crashes,* Basic Books, Inc, 1978

- Mackay, Charles, *Extraordinary Popular Delusions and the Madness of Crowds,* Farrar, Straus & Giroux, 1932

- Galbraith, John Kenneth, *A Short History of Financial Euphoria,* Whittle Direct Books, 1990

- Mauldin, John, *Bull's Eye Investing,* John Wiley & Sons, 2004

ABOUT THE AUTHORS

Randy R. Beeman

Co-founder of the Wise Investor Group at RW Baird in Reston, Virginia.

Randy has more than 15 years of experience in managing financial assets for individuals and corporations. He has also built entrepreneurial business ventures from start-up to eventual sale and has provided accounting services for public firms and private corporations.

Randy is an author, lecturer, and host of "The Wise Investor Show" heard at 9 a.m. ET every Sunday on WMAL 630 AM in Washington, DC. He also hosts the Wednesday "Midweek Update" podcast on iTunes and at www.thewiseinvestorgroup.com.

Randy received his BS in Accounting from the University of Maryland and his MBA in Finance from Shenandoah University in Winchester, Virginia. He lives with his family in Loudoun County, Virginia.

James D. Schneider

James joined the Wise Investor Group in 2000 as an equity research analyst and is now a Vice President specializing in equity securities, macroeconomics and assisting in asset allocation selection in client portfolios. He holds a BS in Finance from George Mason University in Virginia. James and his wife live in Herndon, Virginia.

ABOUT THE WISE INVESTOR GROUP

Co-founded by Randy Beeman, the Wise Investor Group at RW Baird is a team of experienced financial planners, portfolio managers, investment analysts, and account service professionals located in Reston, Virginia. The group provides discretionary asset management services for individuals, employee retirement plans, and endowments. Under Randy's leadership, the group manages more than $1.7 billion in equity, balanced, and fixed-income accounts.

What we can do for you:

As a Baird branch office, we draw on the skills and experience of a broader team of experts throughout Baird to deliver comprehensive financial solutions and customized strategies, helping ensure that our recommendations and approaches are deeply researched and up-to-the-minute. Our reputation and growth are derived from our commitment to expert advice and tailored personal service.

Guided by a value-oriented management style, the Wise Investor Group team of experienced financial professionals will help you build a comprehensive wealth management strategy through personalized financial planning, portfolio management, and in-depth analysis. We believe in a disciplined, value-based investment management strategy. By taking a long-term, conservative investment approach, our clients can better weather market swings in pursuit of financial security.

HONORS AND AWARDS:

2010

- *Barron's*: One of "The Top 100 Financial Advisors" in the United States, April 19, 2010
- *Barron's*: Ranked #3 in Virginia, "The Top 1,000 Advisors: State-by-State," February 22, 2010

2009

- *Barron's*: One of "The Top 100 Financial Advisors" in the United States, April 20, 2009
- *Barron's*: Ranked #1 in Virginia, "The Top 1,000 Advisors: State-by-State," February 9, 2009
- *Virginia Business Magazine*: 2009 Waiting For Recovery: Top Adviser in Virginia

2008

- *Virginia Business Magazine*: 2008 Virginia's Top Wealth Advisers Ranked #2
- *Research Magazine*: "Top Ranked Advisor Teams in America," September, 2008

LISTEN IN:

- "The Wise Investor Show" is broadcasted live every Sunday on WMAL AM 630, Washington, DC, 9:00-10:00 a.m. Eastern Standard Time or www.wmal.com
- Wednesday iTunes "Midweek Update" podcast, which is also on www.thewiseinvestorgroup.com

CONTACT US:

The Wise Investor Group
Robert W. Baird & Co.
11951 Freedom Drive, Suite 1000
Reston, VA 20190
www.thewiseinvestorgroup.com
(866)758-WISE (9473)

Value Returns

Value Returns

For more information about the
Value Returns book visit,

www.valuereturns.com
http:twitter.com/valuereturns

Value Returns